IS IT JUST ME?

ALSO BY WHOOPI GOLDBERG

Alice

Book

Whoopi's Big Book of Manners

SUGAR PLUM BALLERINAS SERIES:

Sugar Plum Ballerinas: Plum Fantastic

Sugar Plum Ballerinas: Toeshoe Trouble

Sugar Plum Ballerinas: Perfectly Prima

Sugar Plum Ballerinas: Terrible Terrel

IS IT JUST ME?

Or is it nuts out there?

WHOOPI GOLDBERG

HYPERION

NEW YORK

Paperback ISBN: 978-1-4013-1065-3

Hyperion books are available for special promotions and premiums. For details
contact the HarperCollins Special Markets Department in the New York office
at 212-207-7528, fax 212-207-7222, or email spsales@harpercollins.com

Book design by Karen Minster

FIRST PAPERBACK EDITION

10 9 8 7 6 5 4 3 2 1

THIS LABEL APPLIES TO TEXT STOCK

We try to produce the most beautiful books possible, and we are also extremely
concerned about the impact of our manufacturing process on the forests of the
world and the environment as a whole. Accordingly, we've made sure that all of
the paper we use has been certified as coming from forests that are managed,
to ensure the protection of the people and wildlife dependent upon them.

To EJ & CJ,
the two most civil folks in my life.

Do unto others
as you would have done unto you.

CONTENTS

Acknowledgments xi

Foreword: Rude Awakening xiii

Abuse It and Lose It 1

Politics Has Gotten #$!@%! Nasty 4

Group Insult 9

Big Blogger 12

If You Can't Be Witty, Don't Be Shitty........................... 15

Then Maybe You Should Stop Complaining 18

Abuse 21

Censorship 23

Road Rude.. 25

SELF-TEST: Parking 28

No Condom? No Way 29

If You Don't Want to Hear the Answer,
   Don't Ask the Question 31

A CIVIL PERSON'S HANDY LIST:
   Things to Tell People Who Put You on the Spot 35

Gracious You 37

Toenail Clipping and Common Scents............................ 40

Where Is the Respect? 44

You Respect My Opinion, I'll Respect Yours 47

A CIVIL PERSON'S HANDY LIST:
   How Not to Turn a Discussion into a Fight 51

Daily Rehab 52

T.S.A. Does Not Mean "Time to Smart Ass" 55

A CIVIL PERSON'S HANDY LIST:
   How Not to Slow Down a TSA Screening................... 60

Just Plane Good Manners 61

Even Steve Jobs Has to Turn Off His Cell Phone 65

SELF-TEST: A Traveler Check.................................... 68

Fragrant Fliers 70

A CIVIL PERSON'S HANDY LIST:
 Stinky Foods Not to Bring on a Plane 72

Babes on a Plane... 75

A CIVIL PERSON'S HANDY LIST:
 What to Bring for a Kid on a Plane 78

Louder, They Can't Hear You in the Lobby........................... 79

A CIVIL PERSON'S HANDY LIST:
 Places Not to Use a Cell Phone 86

Thank You for Not Texting 87

SELF-TEST: Resisting Textation 91

A Flea on the Ass of a Mosquito 93

Play Nice or Stay Home 96

SELF-TEST: Stadium Behavior 99

Block That Parent.. 101

SELF-TEST: Sideline Civility.................................. 103

Down in Front! 105

Manners 107

An Elevator Is Like a Bathroom 109

Encourage Your Kids to Play by Themselves 112

Peer Itself 114

Role Models Will Disappoint You 118

A CIVIL PERSON'S HANDY LIST:
 Role Models Who Have Disappointed Us 121

How Do I Look? And Tell the Truth 123

The Three Questions 126

You Realize I Can See You 128

If You Don't Like It, Don't Do It................................. 131

Should We Be Worried About This? 135

Bloggers Are Cowards 139

Don't Think You Know Someone
Because You See Them on Television.................................... 142

A CIVIL PERSON'S HANDY LIST:
Commonly Used Hurtful Words and Phrases 145

You Realize I Can Hear You 146

The Smarter Things to Say 150

SELF-TEST: Offensive Language... 151

Think It, Don't Say It 152

A CIVIL PERSON'S HANDY LIST:
Things to Think and Not Say.. 154

Buddy Is the New Nigger... 155

Just Because I'm a Catholic,
Don't Assume That a Priest Has Touched Me 157

There Aren't Enough Jails.. 160

Take Your Stinking Paws Off Me,
You Damned Dirty Ape!... 165

A CIVIL PERSON'S TRULY HANDY LIST:
The Hands-Off List.. 167

A CIVIL PERSON'S HANDY LIST:
Behavior to Avoid in the Workplace 168

Simple Requests for Portraying Black People............................ 170

Questions You Should Ask
a Week Before Guests Come to Your House 171

Who Rules When It's Not Your House?....................................... 172

Noisy Neighbors.. 175

Bullies 177

SELF-TEST: Am I a Bully? 186

Manners Don't Take a Vacation.. 188

May I Have Your Attention Please? . . . *Please?* 190

Stress One Now 192

With All Due Respect 194

Master Score Sheet for Self-Tests 195

Glossary of Terms & Other Words.. 197

ACKNOWLEDGMENTS

First, I want to acknowledge Tom Straw because without him I would not have been able to have had this done on time.

I want to thank all the folks at Hyperion, including Gretchen Young and Ellen Archer, for taking a chance on this book. I know it may irritate some people and I don't care (just kidding). I would also like to thank all the folks at WME, especially Cara Stein and Suzanne Gluck. Also, Tom Leonardis, my business partner, and Shannon Schmidt who's in our office. And, I want to thank all the folks who were kind enough to give me things that made them crazy—this is for all of you. Lastly, thanks to my cat, Oliver, who rubbed up against my legs at the right time.

Foreword:
Rude Awakening

First of all, thanks for picking up this book. I'm sure the cover got your attention too. That was the point. Now that you've done so, you may be wondering, "What the hell?"—which is one of the names I had for this. Some of the others were *Uncivil Liberties* (which no one got), or *If You're in Confession, You Can't Have an Autograph*, which everyone said sounded like a prissy book by a celebrity. And then *Is It Just Me?* came into being because it really does say it all.

As it turns out, it isn't just me. When I asked different people what was bugging them, it turned out that it was the same stuff bugging me!—and I knew what I wanted to write.

Somehow so many little pieces of courtesy have gone by the wayside. People in your face, in your business, not caring if they are invading your space, being disrespectfully loud.

Thoughtlessness is the new manners, and I've got to say I don't like it. Now, I'm guilty of some of those things, but I'm aware of it, so I try not to share my cell phone conversations with everyone. I try to remember to say "please" and "thank you"—all the things my mom taught me to do . . . that I don't do anymore. But if I'm slacking on it, and if you're slacking on it, and everyone else is slacking on it, well, you can see just how we may have gotten ourselves to the point of "I'm Annoyed/You're Annoyed."

So over the last year there were days when I remembered to write things down that struck me. Many are written here. They cover the map of my mind, unleashed on you the way they appear in my head. Little things, the way I can comment on them in a book but not on TV.

In no particular order—oh, and I don't necessarily have any answers guaranteed to work for anyone. I can just hear you saying, "Jeez, Whoop, your head's up your butt," or "Hey, Whoop, that's interesting." But either way, you might as well get this book 'cause that guy over there just sneezed and didn't cover his mouth, and the look on your face says, "No, Whoop, it's not just you."

Whoopi
East Coast
May 12, 2010

IS IT JUST ME?

Abuse It and Lose It

People do a lot of crazy things, but when I think about all of the things they should not be doing, the craziest thing on my mind is people drinking and driving.

How long have we been trying to stop drunk driving? Oh, only for as long as I can remember. Think of all those films they made us watch back in driver's ed. And then there's all the public service announcements on TV. I always wondered why they play them late at night, though, while the drinkers are still in the bars getting tanked. Oh well. But when it comes to drunk driving, you can't say there isn't awareness. What's missing is effectiveness.

Maybe the ads aren't graphic or scary enough. At least not enough to reach the people who get hammered and drive. Now, for smoking, it's different. I see thousands of TV commercials showing people stuck in bed because they smoke cigarettes and they're dying of cancer. They make these heart-wrenching pleas, "Don't be like me . . . Don't smoke." It's impossible to watch them and not feel the impact emotionally. Unless I'm missing something, I don't see any PSAs as powerful about drinking and driving. I don't see anybody doing any commercials with the cars burned up and turned to charcoal . . . blood spatters all over the ground . . . some celebrity announcer getting all whispery, saying, had this driver not had that final drink then he or she would still be alive.

But the more I think about it, the sad truth is, maybe no public service announcement—no matter how strong or scary—is going to be enough. After all, disturbing as they are, I've seen plenty of those stop smoking spots, and I still light up.

I think we need to do more.

This subject has always been in my consciousness for one reason. It's basic. I believe that people have to be responsible for what they do. There's a concept, huh? Personal responsibility. Good lord, Whoopi's gone crazy, talking like that!

It's true, though. Actions should have consequences. But the consequences also have to match the responsibility. So, all right, then. If I smoke, I know there's a possibility that I could croak from it. I also know there's a possibility I could croak just because I stepped on the sidewalk. But what I don't like is that I can drink and drive and get caught—and then get my car back!! That's not a consequence. If I drink and drive, if I get pulled over and flunk the test, my car should be taken. Period. That's a consequence. You shouldn't get two, or three, or four, five, six chances.

Now, remember the woman who was that wrong-way driver on the Taconic Parkway in New York? Yeah, who could forget. Well, there's still a lot of talk about her because her husband says he didn't know her to be a drug user or an alcohol abuser. Folks in her neighborhood were kind of saying the same thing. And yet her stomach contents told a totally different story. If the lab tests were correct, though, you have to wonder, was this a one-time thing? We will never really know. But we do know this: For a lot of drunk drivers, it doesn't happen just once. Not even close. But, hold on, if so many people get caught drinking and driving, and then go out and do it again and again and again, it begs the question: Why is it?

I'll tell you why.

Because there's no consequence.

Oh, sure there are penalties, but not enough to be a deterrent. Not from what I've seen. Not happening. The evidence is that the behavior continues. How many times do we see that drunk drivers like the guy who allegedly killed Nick Adenhart, the Angels baseball player, *are repeat offenders*? Hey, why did that dude still have a car? He should *not* have been able to have a car. No debate. You don't want people to drink and drive? When they do it—take the car! And then they have to prove that they're clean and able to be a responsible human being behind the wheel.

I tell you, if I had my own world? If you drank and drove, and got caught, you would not have a car. Your new best friend would be the bus, Jack. Someone would have to come and get you from the police station. And you would not be able to get your car back until I knew that you had gone through a program and had a certificate that said you have been clean and sober for seventy-five days.

And while I'm good and hot about this, let me unload on the texters. If you get caught texting, your car should disappear for a month. Because, you know what? It's too dangerous to text and drive, same as drinking. You get caught . . . bye-bye, car. You're not a responsible enough person.

Some people might say that is too extreme. Come on. If you're not going to be responsible, someone has to step in like when you were a kid. The minute you're doing something that is affecting the public roadways or other places where you can do harm to others, I don't care if the government steps in and takes your car. You shouldn't have been drinking and driving.

And if a public service message won't get your attention, maybe that will.

Politics Has Gotten
#$!@%! Nasty

If you're involved in politics, first of all, let me say this. I feel sorry for you. Seriously. How do people manage to get up every day and do that job? I don't get it. I just don't see how. And it's always been a tough business. You have to have one thick hide, I don't care what party you are in.

And being President doesn't cut you any slack. Not one bit. No matter what a President does, the other side is going to say, "We don't want it." Now, that sort of comes with the turf when you have more than one political party. It's why guys like Stalin and Hitler didn't need to do too much debating. Or vote-counting. Campaign spending? Not an issue. We have give and take. That's at the heart of what's always made our country work, I think. Your side didn't always win, but you shook hands and moved on. It's never been perfect, but mostly, it's been good for the people.

But things have changed. It feels like politics today is not about what's best for the people. Politics today seems to be about my side shoulda won—and we're going to do everything we can do to make you look bad.

And wow, do they ever.

Once, when you heard a politician say it was time to roll up our sleeves, it meant to get down to business. Now it's for the fight. What the hell is going on? Senators flipping people off. Congressmen heckling the President, shouting that he lies. Political negativity has become toxic.

I could never go into politics. I don't have the patience. I would have popped that guy from South Carolina that yelled

"You lie!" right there in Congress. I'm tired of the disrespect that's being shown to the office. I'm tired of people saying, "Well, we're not going to let our kids listen to the President of the United States." How do you not play his address to the children? What's the message you're sending? Is it really that you don't like his politics?

Hey, while we're at it? I'm also tired of people asking him for his birth certificate. Maybe they'd also like two forms of photo ID so he can cash a check while he's at it . . . Yeah, like they'd ever cash his check.

Presidents have always had their detractors, but come on. Was there ever this degree of pissing-on-trees acrimony around President Clinton or President Bush?

So what is it? Is it politics? Race? What is it?

Hard question. I go back and forth about what it is. I know what it sounds like.

But if I were President . . . which would never happen . . . but let's say for these purposes here—let's say if I *were* the President—I would say to that heckler, "I am the President of the United States. You may not like all my policies. You may not like what I stand for, but you don't get to disrespect me. We are a civil society. We're not Parliament, OK?"

But I'd say it an inch from his face . . . But I wouldn't shout. Because A, I'm not a hypocrite, and B, I'm too cool to stoop.

So what's the deal? Is it race, or a total lack of acceptance in the turnout of the election? To make matters worse, all the talking heads have been incredibly disrespectful on both sides. There's never been a shortage of partisan goons to push everybody's buttons, but never like this before. This feels different.

Debates that used to be about finger-pointing are all about finger-biting. Middle-aged folks are disrupting town hall meetings. Tea Party people are taking their tea bagging to the streets . . . People are scared. It's kooky.

A few years back, when I appeared at a rally for John Kerry, I made this joke . . . I'm a comic, after all. It started this ugly storm of controversy. You may or may not remember all that, but if you do, let me ask you something. Did you ever see what I said?

No, nobody did. Because if you go back to those newspapers right after the incident, try to find what I said.

Go ahead. I want you to see if you can find what I actually said. Here's a big hint: You won't see it.

It was a joke about Bush. But all of the newspapers that said that I said something terrible never actually printed what I said. That drove me crazy. It made it sound worse because it was left to folks' imaginations. They print other controversial things. There's a way to do that. You know, whenever someone curses or is crude . . . what they do in print is put in some dots and dashes. "He's a big old P-dot-dash-exclamation-point-Y." That's what you would see.

We saw it when Vice President Biden whispered his F-bomb to the president at the signing ceremony for the health care bill and he didn't know his microphone was live. Good ol' Joe. He's the cool uncle who sort of has this Restless Lip Syndrome. Whether you like his politics or not, that guy always keeps things entertaining. And when he leaned in to whisper in the President's ear, all the TV stations and the newspapers used the punctuation trick when they quoted him saying, "This is a big f***ing deal."

Not the case with me.

No one took a moment to say, "Well, where is it? Where is the quote? What exactly did she say?" And here's the real pisser. Even if I said something about the President, when did that become a no-no?

I've messed with Presidents from Reagan to Obama. Although . . . to be clear . . . I never once heckled them. And certainly not in a joint session of Congress. Puh-leeze!

Do you see there's a difference? I comment. I skewer. I joke. That's part of what I do as a comic. And it's a cornerstone of America's First

Amendment rights. I mean, we're not in Iran or China, where it is courting death. So what was the result? It became economically unfeasible to make any protest or comment. It also got very vindictive, and I got no support from Democrats who were there.

As I think about it, maybe it was the beginning of what we're seeing more of now.

Which takes me right back to why I would never run for President. I wouldn't. And know why? Same reason a lot of folks don't. Or who don't go for cabinet appointments or judgeships.

Who the hell wants to be subjected to all the prying? Ask yourself. If you had the shot, would you want all your business hanging out there like that? I hear you. Who would?

Let he who is without sin run for office, because everyone else would never pass the test. Or put up with it.

Too bad. It would be nice to have more people running our government who have lived different lives. But we've made it impossible for those people to step forward. There's too much scrutiny. First your bank accounts get pawed through. Then they start pontificating about your affiliations with subversive groups. You know, like AAA and Sam's Club. And suddenly, some distant cousin finds himself as the lead story on the news. Why? Because someone investigating you ended up discovering poor old cuz smoked pot in college. And what really upsets you is that he never shared.

And then there was that library book you checked out on— gasp!—human anatomy. Hey, judging from what most politicians are into these days, at least it was humans.

The whole process is a barrage of invasiveness. What have you done? Who did you do it with? . . . And then there's all those forms to fill out.

Now, of course, I am not perfect. I am *really* imperfect.

That's why I'll never run for office. Because you have to be too clean. I am not clean. I've had a lot of mud. Forget the skeletons,

I've got the mud. And, know what? I don't want to have to explain me to anybody.

I think we're all better off with me here on the sidelines, doing me.

Group Insult

Let me see . . . We've had the New Deal. We've had the Great Society. I think this era has a name too. Know what I think it is? I think it's the Fugliness. And not because of all the bad plastic surgery out there. I call it that because politicians aren't just ugly with each other. Now it's whole groups of folks . . . and often, the politicians won't come out and say who they are talking about—like Arizona. In Arizona, they keep saying "illegal aliens," but to me, that's ALL illegals . . . British, Italian, Greek, Africans, Chinese, Canadians . . . It's a long list of those not here legally. So let's find them. Make them go through the process, right? I'm down for that.

However, that's NOT what they mean in Arizona. They mean Mexicans, so why not have the balls to say what they mean? Come out and say, "We want the right to check the papers of anyone WE think might be an illegal Mexican." Because if they had to look at those words, they would have to look at their own BS—and see themselves the same way we see the Nazi period when they did a similar thing.

Or how about when they talk about the welfare system and they always just love to flash somebody's picture up abusing welfare in some flamboyant way. Like folks all over the country are just sitting around drinking and partying—enjoying the good life on the dole.

Ahh . . . nothing like it.

Guess what? People on welfare generally don't want to be there. They want to get off welfare.

But, you see, politicians like to label groups in order to manipulate public opinion to their way of thinking. And nothing gets attention faster than demonizing somebody. Put a face on the problem, but don't leave off the devil horns! They say, "Oh, look at those people over there collecting fifteen checks and beating the system, taking money out of your pocket." Well, yeah, there are people who are doing that. There are people who did that in the white-collar sector too. It's not just welfare recipients that double-dip.

How about Enron, or Bernie Madoff, or any of those Wall Street bailout guys who were broke but still throwing lavish parties? Want to talk about abusing a system? The bill for the ice sculptures at those parties was higher than that junk mortgage they sold you. But we don't feel like they're the ones doing it to us. Somehow when talk turns to people on welfare, they're the culprits, they're the people who are screwing us. It's always, "We were able to make it. Why can't they?" . . . Which sounds a whole lot like, "I have my ice sculpture, where's yours?"

But I think that's probably changed a lot now since the recession. Because I think people started to see that unexpected things come up, and folks can't be so certain where they're going to be. And if that's you, you want there to be a safety net in place. You want the welfare system to be there for you. The whole reason for these programs is to help when the unexpected happens—to anyone.

Like health care. I'm glad that the coverage passed. Because the truth of the matter is none of us knows when we're going to need it. And all those folks who say, no, no, we're never going to need it, they have to take a look at what's going on. Who ever thought they were going to lose their job? You worked for folks and you thought you had a lifelong job with them. No more.

So because nobody knows if they themselves are going to end up needing assistance, I'd be very cautious before I insulted a whole group of people over stories you see about the bad apples taking cruises and drinking champagne in welfare hot tubs.

Like I said, there are those people, they do exist. But, come on. We all know a small percentage of frauds don't make up the entire system. It's like pregnancy. Pregnant teenagers don't make up that entire picture. Black people on welfare don't make up that entire picture. Most folks don't realize the people who benefited most from Affirmative Action were women . . . and white women were topping the list. Why? Because they were able to go into the work force and into colleges in a way that they'd never been able to before. They are the biggest recipients of Affirmative Action—women! But when you listen to people talk about Affirmative Action, it's all, "Oh . . . all those black kids . . . getting everything just handed to them." So you've got to pay attention. 'Cause there's a lot of information out there that is sort of semi-right but not totally.

And here's something else. I know what I'm talking about when I talk about the value of welfare because I was on it.

And thank God for the welfare system.

It helped me through a very tough time. When I went on it, I knew I was going to get a job eventually. And when I did get on my feet, I sent the check back. Yup. I didn't need it. I wrote a little note that I put in with it and said, "I've managed to get myself some work and I don't think I'll be needing these anymore. So please remove me from the roll."

Many people do that, send their last checks back.

You don't hear about that from detractors, do you? No, because detractors don't care about the facts. That's the saddest part about so many things. Facts no longer seem to matter. And then when the truth comes out, it's way the hell back on page ninety with little, tiny, unreadable print.

They save the big type for the insults. Why? Because every cause needs a demon.

Big Blogger

Look at you there. Sitting back, quietly holding this book. Know what you're doing? You are enjoying something so rare, you might not recognize it. Know what it is?

You are having a private moment.

Is it just me, or does it seem there is no such thing as a private life anymore? Big Brother is here watching you. Except he's doing it through his blog instead of some science fiction telescreen. Hey, forget the government. This ass-kicking our privacy is getting comes at the exact same time regular folks have lost any sense of respecting a personal boundary. Personal boundaries . . . pardon me while I get nostalgic. Ahhh . . . those were quaint times, weren't they?

Hey, and in case you're wondering, this isn't some boo-hoo from some whiny celebrity. Check yourself. It doesn't matter if you are famous or not. Not with YouTube and Facebook and Twitter and all the other things that are out there now. It's the same for everyone. There is no privacy. And we brought this on ourselves.

Cell phones. Man, have cell phones changed the game. How? Simple. They have cameras and video on them.

Anything I do or anywhere I go, someone with a cell phone is there to take a picture or to pick up something I am overheard saying, and then it can be taken out of context. And after it happens, I've learned there's no point in clarifying. People don't want to listen.

It feels like people don't want you at your best, they want you at your worst. That's where we've been heading. I guess it makes other people feel better about their own lives.

That's why I'm going off on this shift away from respecting boundaries. We haven't just crossed them. We've crossed them, kicked dirt on them, obliterated the lines, and then let the dog come take a pee on them. They're gone, baby, gone.

Not long ago in Manhattan, a blog did an instant posting. "Whoopi's in the Apple store." People showed up.

And they chased me.

I don't like that. Does that surprise you? It lets people driving around looking for me know where I am. Or anybody who wants to do me any harm. Why do they get to do that? Why does some anonymous goofball get to print my whereabouts? It seems wrong on so many levels.

But it's not going to change, so, all right, you make a decision to deal with it. You make it work.

Michael Jackson did that. Michael couldn't go to an amusement park. So he built an amusement park inside his velvet prison.

We live in prisons of our own making.

Where do I get my freedom? In a book. On my couch, farting. Eating Wise Potato Chips. Not having to make any explanation to anybody about how many I'm eating or why I'm still smoking.

Home. That's my freedom.

What is yours? I sure hope you are able to enjoy whatever it is. Because if you are not a famous person and think you are immune, think again. Anything can come back and bite you if you put it out there on Twitter.

People out there—ex-lovers, business rivals, bosses, coworkers, former schoolmates harboring a grudge you forgot about long ago—don't always have your best interests at heart. Something you said or did—innocently, even—a long time ago on a video or in a picture can come back to haunt you.

It's easy now for private things to be made public, and when you say or do what you feel in a public space, prepare yourself, my friend. Hear my warning. You can no longer be surprised by the result. And there's no space more public than the Internet.

It might be cute to get drunk and take your top off in Venice. Woo-hoo, right? But if you put a picture of that out on the Web for your friends, you have no control over who else sees it—or what happens to it after you post it. Or what happens if the friends stop being friends. That put a little ice in your blood, didn't it?

Listen, the only place you should have nude pictures of yourself is at your house. No one else should be able to look at that. Unless they come to your house and you show them. Woo-hoo.

And, heads up. If you are willing to stay in a job that you hate, and have all sorts of things to say about how bad it is and what monsters they are—sure, tell your friends. But do it privately. Don't post it on the Internet.

Because nothing is anonymous anymore. There are no secrets anymore. And if it can come back to bite you on the ass, it will.

Now everything's online. But no one asked me if I want my private information on the Internet.

Did they ask you?

If You Can't Be Witty, Don't Be Shitty

OK, here's what I want to know. What makes somebody get up in the morning and think that they can criticize what clothes you put on that day? I mean, really. Why do casual coworkers think you and I are fair game for their fashion assessment? "Hey, second time I've seen those pants this week." "That sweater has an interesting texture. What is it, ShamWow?" "Helen, is that blouse a little young for you?"

What???

Baby, you have a false sense of intimacy. Have you looked in the mirror? Are you really close enough to me or any other person to say something like that and know that your mouth isn't hurting their feelings? Are the objects of your ridicule close enough to you to be allowed to do the same thing to you?

Uh-huh . . . didn't think so.

These people have no license to critique what we have on. But that's not bad enough. They try to make a joke out of it. Notice I say "try," because most times? It's not even a funny one. This assumed intimacy they have is pure fantasy. Time to wake up. Hey, fashion comic: We are not intimate. Just because we work together doesn't instantaneously make you my friend. Or my comedy cohort.

Most people don't know how to be funny. Or witty. That is still an art form. So they attempt humorous critiques that end up coming off cruel. Funny is hit or miss sometimes, especially when it's at the expense of other people. Last I checked, funny is to make folks laugh, not send them crying to the bathroom.

Here's the thing. Unless you have a relationship with someone, do not say anything about their apparel unless it's useful. Like your pants are on fire. Because I would want to know that . . . Otherwise, keep walking.

When I first hit the movie scene, I took a lot of flak for my style, my dreads, my clothes—for being myself. Hey, pretty much, I've always just been me. And I guess I have proved myself correct in staying true to who I am. Don't think I could do it any other way. Want to know what I think fashion is all about? Real fashion is the fashion of my soul.

But looking back, I think perhaps some folks just weren't ready for me. Think of what Hollywood was all about. They'd never had any experience with anyone like me. Or who looked like me or who sounded like me. So they had to sort of deal with their own issues on race and hair and what's beautiful and what isn't beautiful.

But I also separate the actor me from the daily me. When you're an actor you have to look different for your role. That makes sense, right? So you put the wigs on, you put the eyebrows on, and do what you're supposed to do to create the right look for your character. Sometimes it's kind of fun doing that kind of dress-up. But once I come out of a role and finish a job, I don't want anybody telling me what I'm supposed to look like. Or tell me that I'm wrong because I look a certain way. Or not the way they think I should be looking.

If I'm not working, I am about one thing and one thing only. I am all about being comfortable. I dress in a way that makes me happy. And for sure not to please others.

Don't get me wrong, I love looking at fashion. I love fashion, I do. But you've got to know this about your friend Whoop. I'm not willing to run, or ride a bike, or exercise, or go to the gym. Not more than twice a year, anyway.

The fact is, I will never be six two. Things I wear will look different on me than someone else. So I wear what I like. I like jeans. I really like jeans. I also like high heels. I love great shoes. So that's what you'll see me in a lot.

Not too long ago there was this thing in *TV Guide* where these two women who I don't know and who don't know me proceeded to talk about what my character was all about based on what I wear. What?? Excuse me? You can't do that. These were just two people making snide remarks. Don't need 'em.

Here's what I say to that. Do not equate my brain with my jeans.

And it's not just me. Remember what the fashion big mouths were saying about Jessica Simpson? Looking at her magazine pictures, sucking their teeth, going, "Oh, look at her in her 'mom jeans.'" Know what? That is an unnecessarily cheap shot at her and kinda lousy to moms at the same time. Who the hell are they to say that? What gratification does it give them to be mean at someone's expense?

People made nasty comments like that about President Obama. They made an issue of his jeans when he threw out the first ball at the All-Star game in St. Louis. Why? Who was he bothering? Come on.

The tabloids, celebrity mags, and TV entertainment shows do fashion critiques all the time. But it's not about fashion, it's about trashin'. Their specialty is "Celebrity Cellulite!"—running unflattering pictures of stars at the beach and saying who should give up the bikini and go for the one-piece. And this is acceptable? This is a mark of journalism in a civil society, to take ambush pictures of people at the beach? And if the camera was turned around and pointed the other way, what would that look like?

Eesh. Don't wanna know.

Maybe these public fashion attacks are what give your close personal pal, the office comedian, the idea that it's all right to riff on what you're wearing. Personally, I'd tell him to save it. Save it for his awesome Borat impression at the company picnic.

Then Maybe You Should Stop Complaining

Look, we all get bugged by stuff people pull on us from time to time. What am I talking about? I'm talking about office gossip. I'm talking about folks trash talking you behind your back. Or stealing credit for something you did. Or making you the goat for something they screwed up.

Oh, that never happens to you? Then you must be independently wealthy from the lottery . . . 'cause the rest of us have to deal.

If someone's behavior is driving you crazy, here's the thing. Recognize that you have options. Here they are. Ready? You can ignore it, you can bitch about it, or you can make an attempt to fix it. It all depends on how badly you want to change the situation.

You can leave it alone and be nervous about it all the time and not ever try to correct it, or you can talk to the person and do something about it. But if it's a matter of, "Oh, I'm too scared to do that," then you don't actually want to change the situation. Sorry, but that's the truth. So what do you do?

Make a decision. What's it worth to you?

Oh, yeah, I know it's going to get ugly. And you kind of have to know what you're getting into when you stir the bees' nest. Take a sec. Pause and examine yourself and see if it's worth the tension if you confront this person. But you also have to ask yourself, is that one moment of tension worse than what you're dealing with on an ongoing basis? Only you know.

Taking action is hard, but know what? Enduring a bad situation can be its own hell. I have a feeling you may already know that.

And when you boil it all down, which is kind of what I'm trying to do for you here . . . these are the basics of everything: How badly do you want it to change . . . and are you willing to act? And the answer to those two questions will guide what direction you take. It will guide your choice of whether or not to talk to this person. Or to your boss, if this is person is a coworker causing a problem. It will also guide *how* you talk. Because if you go in and you're belligerent, you might not get the result you were hoping for. In fact, I can sort of guarantee it. So count to three and think.

Now, if you decide you're just going to ignore this situation and live with it? Cool. But stop bitching about it. Really. Otherwise, you know what you are in danger of becoming? One of those annoying people who is a chronic complainer who doesn't do anything to change the problem.

And then we'll all have to work up the courage to talk to you!

You have a choice to make, and it is all yours.

If your decision is to confront it—if that is right for your particular situation and you can cope with the consequences—you've got to say clearly what, in your mind, happened. Speak your facts. It's all about what you say.

And how you say it.

Here's what I'd do. Start thinking about how it all ends. That's right. Ask yourself, "What result do I want from this?" Now, don't blow past this. That is worth some careful thought. So many people finally seize a moment but then just barge in with mouths blazing and no goal. Big mistake. Usually, all that does is dig a deeper hole. Sit quietly first and think. Pretend you got the outcome you wanted. What *is* it? OK, now, work toward that and forget everything else. I'm here to tell you, it is so much more effective than just attacking. Anybody can do that.

Seek a result. And that starts by envisioning what it is.

And have your facts straight. When you know you are right, it's very easy to say, "Look, here's what I actually said," or "Here's why what you're hearing about me is wrong." But do make sure you have your facts right, because it makes every bit of difference if you are not standing on thin ice.

Got a big old iceberg under your feet? Good for you! Go for it.

Abuse

Nobody has the right to put rough hands on you. You do understand that, don't you? It's a given. It's wrong. It's also illegal. But people in relationships do it all the time. And people, usually women, find themselves trapped in a world of abuse.

Now, I'll admit to you that this is a big subject. A very big subject that's worth a book in itself, not just a chapter. But, see, this is my shot to share with you, so if you are in an abusive relationship, I want to say something. And it's the same thing that I say about everything:

Make a decision. Because if you've made a decision that you can't do anything about your situation, you won't.

If you have children and you're allowing that to happen to you and your kids . . . it's not that you can't change your circumstances; you won't.

And I don't care what your background is. I don't care what kind of relationship your parents had. None of that matters. Only one thing does.

You have to make a decision. Do you want to get hit? Do you care if your kids get hit? To me, it's black and white. And people say, "Well, no, I can't leave."

You can. And you have to. Or you're going to be dead.

Oh, I hear what you're saying. You're looking at that scary step, saying life will be harder in a lot of ways if you take it. You want it to be easy, but it's just not going to be. You may have to start again. You may have to go in a different direction. But you've got to do it. You're in a bad relationship. You're in a physically bad relationship. I'd rather be angry and upset in a different state.

Escape. Yes, it's a bold move. You leave your job. You go start somewhere else. And when you get to the state that you're driving to, you go directly to the family services and say, "I just left an abusive relationship and I need help." Period.

But you have to make a decision. It's the only way. You *have* to make the decision.

Help yourself a little by making a plan. If you've gone to work and you have a car there, pick the kids up after school—make sure you've packed the car first, if you can do that—and leave. Leave everything you know. The kids are not going to be happy. They're going to be mad at you because of all their friends. It's not worth losing your teeth or your life.

Move.

You have to do it. You've got to do it. You. Can't. Stay.

Now. If that abusive person's with you 24/7, you need to creatively find a way to get to the police station. And if that person leaves you alone for a minute? You've got to seize that opportunity and go. Escape. It's not a discussion. It's not a question. No one has the right to put their hands on you. Nobody.

Know something? I have had friends in these bad relationships and they've asked me what to do about it, and I've said, "You've got to go." And they say, "I can't." And I say, "You would not let anybody do to your kids what is being done to you. So why are you letting that person do it to you? Is it OK because he only does it when he's mad, or when he's drunk? No!"

You're not going to make it better. You're not going to change the person. You can't stay there. It's not going to change. Until you do.

But don't say you can't. Because you can.

Censorship

OK, this may shock you, but I don't think the language I use is inappropriate. All right, maybe it would be in church. But this is me. This is just how I talk, and I've never looked at it as inappropriate. So the things that seem to freak other people out, don't freak me out. It works the other way too. The words that freak me out generally don't freak others out.

Sort of makes life interesting for all of us, huh?

Want to know what words really freak me out? They aren't the curse words. Nope. The words that go up my ass are "stupid" and "dummy." Know why? Because you can't say either of those words with a smile. If you're somebody who doesn't like my curse words, I get it, that's fine. Tell you what. I'll make a little pact with you. When they remove "stupid" from the English language, or "dummy" from the English language, I will temper my "fucks" and "shits." But until then? Not gonna happen.

What I am about to say I *know* freaks people out:

I would love to teach every kid to say "fuck." Hang on, now, hang on, listen to why. The reason is because to me, that is a word that doesn't have any effect. But "stupid" and "dummy"? You can say it to someone who is six and you can say it to someone who is a hundred and six and they will hunch their shoulders and it will be like somebody kicked them in the stomach because they are harsh, ugly words.

"You're so stupid." Man, they say it on TV, they say it as jokes, they say it in the movies, they say it in the commercials, kids say it to each other, and it's a horrific word. And to me, the ugliest, most reprehensible word in the English language is "stupid." So, yes, I understand a lot of people don't get my love of verbiage. But maybe if they could pause and take a look at it my way, I bet of all the words that hurt them—I mean really, really hurt them—they'd realize that "fuck" just isn't one of them.

Look, I enjoy my freedom. And I enjoy my freedom with those words. When it makes other people uncomfortable they say, "Whoopi, you'd be so much smarter if you didn't do it that way." Well, it's possible, sure. But guess what? I like the way I do it. And if you have noticed anything about me over the years, you may have an inkling that I'm not about to stop. So if you are one of those people, you have a choice to make. You can either hear what I have to say, and maybe hear some of those words—and know that they are words that I love because they have no harm in them—or don't. And maybe miss out on something that might be kind of fun or smart. But the choice is always yours.

Road Rude

I don't want anyone killing me with their car. Is that too much to ask? No, it's not. Then why are so many people trying to send me to my early reward with their vehicles? Truly. I can't believe some of the stunts I see pulled out there on the road. I have to say the worst behavior you see from people is when they get a steering wheel in their hands. To the point that I believe that your car is like a brain scan of your personality.

If you are a polite person or just a normal, considerate, going-along-and-along-in-life person, that's pretty evident. You get a smile and a nod from me at the next stoplight.

If you are easily distracted, clumsy, or kind of off in the ozone, we're going to see that too. Please try to keep it off the sidewalk.

And if you are a jackass? Well, trust me, we know. We all know. And the way you carry on, we get plenty of opportunities to confirm that.

Do you think that when you get inside your car and close the door you become magically invisible? You do not. Not even with those tinted windows you think look so cool. We can see you. And it ain't pretty.

Some folks will surprise you when you see what they pull on the highway. These are the people who may not show signs of aggression or rudeness or risky behavior sitting in the break room with you at work, or selling you a nice pair of shoes at the department store. But don't be fooled. It doesn't mean that it's not part of their personality. Like that famous cartoon folks saw in driver's ed. It's where good ol' Goofy gets behind the wheel and suddenly becomes Satan. That's what happens to some people. Folks turn on that ignition, and suddenly, Satan rules.

What makes that happen? Maybe somebody chewed them out just before they left the factory, or they learned in the parking lot that some dude from the marketing department got the promotion they wanted. Or their girlfriend cheated on them. Or their boyfriend refuses to ask his best bud from college to find a motel for the weekend so they can have some alone time.

Or. Or. Or.

Does it matter what reason people have to be misbehaving behind the wheel? Hell, no. Screw the reason, all I care about is how they drive. And if you are a person who acts out with bad behavior behind the wheel, I have a message for you.

If you speed through a school zone, I have a message for you.

If you park in handicapped spaces, I have a message for you.

If you weave through cars on the interstate like it was your personal slalom, I have a message for you.

If you zip into a parking spot that somebody else has been patiently waiting for, I have a message for you.

If you run lights, or bust a crosswalk with people in it, I have a message for you.

If other, more reasonable people obey the law and common sense and pull to the right to let a fire truck or an ambulance pass, and you use that opportunity to pass them all because you think you're so special that doesn't apply to you, I have a message for you.

If you tailgate, practice road rage, live on your horn, pollute with your smoky tailpipe, blind people with your high beams, dent somebody's fender and drive off, throw litter out the car window, drink, text, or watch videos on your cell phone while you should be driving, I have a message for you.

You're looking at it.

Parking

Have you ever parked illegally in a Handicapped Only space?
    If yes, score 5
    If no, score 0

Did you care that you did?
    If yes, score 1
    If no, score 5

Is it bothering you that you did?
    If yes, score 1
    If no, score 5

Is it possible that you prevented someone who needed it from using it?
    If yes, score 5
    If no, score 5

Did you care?
    If yes, score 1
    If no, score 5

Would it piss you off if they did it to you?
    If yes, score 2
    If no, score 5

Total score: _____

Tally your score and write it in on the Master Score Sheet
at the back of this book, page 195.

No Condom? No Way

Unless you're looking to get pregnant, let's talk about common sense.

This behavior is not about etiquette. It's about life-death behavior.

Unless you're looking to get pregnant, or you're looking to catch whatever somebody might have caught that you don't know about—"Put the condom on" should be the first thing out of your mouth. This is not a conversation. There is no debate. If you do not want to get pregnant, the man needs to wear a condom, it's that simple.

Or you don't need to have sex.

It's not a *maybe I should*, or *maybe I shouldn't*. It's very simple. There are things out there that can kill you. If you have this partner and you don't know anything about him, don't do him unless he is wearing a condom, period.

Duh!

And I don't see why it's hard to say, "Stop. I need the condom because I don't want to raise your kids."

And guys, don't be an ass. You should not only wear the condom—invest in the company!

DO NOT make your partner feel bad for asking you to wear it again and again. Or hear you whine that it doesn't feel natural, blah-blah-blah. Both of you say, "OK. We'll find another kind." But you're wearing one. Period.

Not wearing one makes no sense to me.

The condom should be part of the ritual. Learn how to put one on him. But you cannot go bare skin to bare skin anymore.

The world has changed. Period. Period, period, period. And I don't care whether you're concerned that your daughter's going to have sex if you start talking to her about using condoms. She may have sex, but you need to help her protect herself.

Have the conversation.

If You Don't Want to
Hear the Answer,
Don't Ask the Question

Everybody knows nobody likes to be criticized. Because sometimes, depending on who's doing it, it feels like an attack.

But the only thing worse than getting criticized is someone
asking for your opinion about something and they give you hell . . .
and you end up with your head handed to you. Now that's bad
manners. And bad behavior.

People say they want your honest opinion. But do they? Or do
they just want to hear the good stuff?

There was a great article recently by a screenwriter named Josh
Olson. It ran in the *Village Voice*. The man was absolutely right. It
was called "No I Won't Read Your Fucking Script." Brilliant!

It was an opinion piece about how aspiring screenwriters ask
him to read their sample scripts and get his comments. Josh Olson
is a respected professional. And the man knows his craft. Anyway,
this article he wrote is sort of an open letter to the amateur writers
out there who are always trying to get someone's critique. These
folks usually hit you up at cocktail parties, or when you're leaving
the restaurant . . . or the hospital. Or when you are trying to forget
about work for an hour. Here's just a taste of what he wrote in the
Voice:

> . . . I simply have no interest in reading your fucking screen-
> play. None whatsoever. If that seems unfair, I'll make you a
> deal.
>
> In return for you not asking me to read your fucking
> script, I will not ask you to wash my fucking car, or take my
> fucking picture, or represent me in fucking court, or take

out my fucking gall bladder, or whatever the fuck it is that you do for a living.

And that's just the beginning.

The point he makes is that it's pretty much a no-win situation to give somebody advice about *anything* they have created or performed. People ask me to read scripts all the time, and I just don't do it. I won't do it.

But why, Whoop . . . ?

Here's why.

Bo-Be-Boo sends me a script to read, and I read it, and I say, "No, it's not for me." Now. Say someone has the same idea, decides to make it, and thinks of me to be in it. Bo-Be-Boo decides to sue me because I'm now accused of stealing that idea and I have to prove that I didn't. A mess? Yes! But . . . if I don't read the script—I mean I don't even open the envelope—there is no issue.

Sometimes people say, come hear me sing. I say, "You know I'm antisocial. I don't go out." People who know me know that I am antisocial, so they stop asking. And then if I show up, they say, "Wow! OK . . ."

But, if I come, please don't ask me how you sound. 'Cause I won't tell you. Come on!!! People don't really want to know. I know from too much experience that even if I say they sound great, they're going to say, "No, really, tell me, how did I sound?" and I say, "You sounded great." And they go, "But . . . ?"

That's when I'm sorry . . . sorry I was ever asked the question. Even sorrier I ever went. I say to myself, "You know what? Now it's too technical. Now you want to know too much. Now . . . where is my coat?"

Sometimes all folks want is a pat on the back. Other times, people just want to know that they did OK. Most times, they're leading you out into a minefield. I don't take that walk. No way. I try to stay on neutral ground. And my favorite word . . . is "swell." Because nobody's sure what it means. "That was . . . swell."

Gah!!

There's another thing going on here. The *real* point is that someone isn't just asking me to read their script. Or to hear them sing. Or to stare at their paintings. They're asking me to tell them something that only *they* should make a decision about. Do they really need my opinion? Not really. They know if they can do this or they can't. My telling them that they can do it doesn't mean anything.

And that is why God created "swell." Thank you, God!

Also, if somebody does take the time and effort to read your work or come see you perform . . . it's a favor. And if you ask them to call on their expertise and give you their perspective . . . whether it's good or bad . . . your only response should be "Thank you." Even if you disagree and want to have a discussion after, I don't care. Your first two words? "Thank you."

You asked for it . . . and they gave it to you. If you're angry or embarrassed, deal with it. Do not fire back at this person. People do it. That happens. A lot. And it is the worst manners in the world. Why would you do that? This person is already in a tough position . . . And know what? It's one you put him in because you asked for this favor.

One of the best criticisms I ever got was from Mike Nichols. While I was running through my one-woman show before we opened on Broadway, he cleared his throat—as only he can do— and he said, "Um, Miss Goldberg . . ." And I said, "Yes, yes, Mr. Nichols?" And he said, "Is there an end to this story? You're just meandering." I said, ". . . Well, yes, there is an end to this story." And he said, "Yes, and you passed it. And so, obviously, you weren't listening to what you were saying because you would have heard the end of your story."

And he was right. I had gotten where I needed to go, and then I was meandering. He was saying pay attention. And I was paying attention to him. That's Mike Nichols. He's like those old E. F. Hutton commercials. When he speaks, actors listen.

But it's really about you paying attention to yourself too, and listening. And being honest with yourself. I try to be. I'm not always. I refuse to believe that I'm not six two. I can tell myself I'm five four all I want to, I don't believe it.

Things to Tell People Who Put You on the Spot

We all get stuck in that awkward place. You get boxed into sitting through a friend's recital, or their improv showcase, or after dinner they drag you into the basement to look at their artwork, which turns out to be sixty oil paintings of toreadors on black velvet.

"Well? What do you think? And be honest."

No! Once more. No! What you do is tell them what they want to hear by letting them hear what they think they are hearing. Meaning? Stay on the fence.

Keep these handy neutral answers in your head and save everybody's night. And feelings. Here's what you can say:

- "Wow . . ."

- "Swell."

- "You did it again."

- "It's all you."

- "It's got you all over it."

- "How do you do it?"

- "You must be so proud of yourself."

- "I couldn't do that."

- "Nobody but you, nobody but you."

- "I think you found yourself."

- "Somebody's been working."

- "I've never seen/heard anything like this."

- "I am speechless."

None of these is really a lie, now, is it? Especially not this one:

- "Know what? I am going to be remembering this moment for a long time."

What do you think of my list? And be honest . . .

Gracious You

We've all seen this, right? A little kid . . . maybe even your kid . . . one who is possibly the most adorable young man on the planet . . . is at his birthday party. He zooms right past the greeting card without even reading it and starts ripping into that gift wrap and ribbon like a grizzly clawing at a picnic cooler. Ribbon's flying, paper's shredding . . . Stand back, everybody! He gets the box open, sees the present, and, as you wait, poised to capture his delight on camera for posterity, the charming little youngster looks up and says, "This isn't the one I wanted."

But, you know, that's kids. Especially if they're very young. They're not polite, and we all know that. But here's the problem. How many times recently have you seen the same thing play out—the ripping at the paper, the tearing open of the gift, and the comment of disappointment—but it's not a kid, it's a grown-up?

And you think to yourself—WTF!??

Here's my feeling about gifts. I like them. Even the worst ones. Because your worst gift might be my favorite gift. No matter what it is, it shows that you care.

If you open a gift from somebody—and they're sitting right there—watch your face. Don't sit there frowning. So it's a toilet paper cozy. All right. But, hey, not just any toilet paper cozy . . . One that someone spent hours knitting. And in this moment—this split second of discovery—all sorts of things are just banging around in your mind. First is, "Now what the hell am I going to do with a toilet paper cozy?!" And then, "My TP doesn't get cold enough to wear a dainty little sweater. And even if it did, I sure don't want my friends coming over, using my bathroom, and thinking that I am the sort of person who needs, desires, or covets a toilet paper cozy!!" Yep. All those thoughts, and more, go racing around your head—but—and this is essential—but . . . under no circumstances let them come flying out of your mouth. And do not—do not—let them show on your face. No, no. This is your moment to shine. This is your chance to win that Oscar or that Tony Award for Best Performance by a Disappointed Recipient. Here's what you do.

Smile. Show some teeth. Say, "Thank you, it's . . . swell!"

If it's the cell phone you wanted but not the right model, do not say, "Oh. I was hoping for the one with more gigs." Nuh-uh. Where are those teeth? There they are. Smile. Say something like "Wow," or make an agreeable sound.

You can do it!

Now. If you are fortunate enough to have some money, and someone who doesn't got you a ten-dollar coupon for a latte, don't make that person who stretched her budget to include you in her giving feel like crap for caring. Try saying how much you'd love a latte right now. You don't need to overact or anything. We all know it's not a new set of tires for your Porsche. Just accept it with thanks and a smile.

Pretend it's you doing the giving. Do you want to hear right that second that the person has one already? Or that it's the wrong color? Or they don't have room to put it anywhere? Or that they suddenly decided they don't like to collect Belgian beer steins anymore and didn't alert the Western Hemisphere?

What they say is true. You shouldn't look a gift horse in the mouth. That's when you have to suck it up. And, yeah, it really is the thought that counts. And to people who think of you, even if they have no taste, it's still a big deal.

Gifts are a tricky thing. Both people are looking for reaction. If you're the one opening the package, it's a chance for someone who cared enough about you to give it to receive a gift in return. Appreciation.

Be gracious. Like I say, pretend it's you.

Toenail Clipping and Common Scents

I fought with myself on this. I've been going round and round asking myself, "Do I really need to say this?" Sadly . . . yes, I do. Because I—not to mention the rest of us who have seen you do this "activity"—have been sufficiently grossed out. So, I will say this.

Listening?

Please, do not cut your toenails on the train. Or on the bus. Or at the table you are hogging at Starbucks. It's not your bathroom.

Do that at home!

And if you find that it takes you too long in the morning to do it there—*get up earlier*. But I don't want to have to sit and look at you doing that. And I am not alone. Oh, and clipping your toenails? That goes with brushing your hair—I don't want to see that in public either.

It's not OK to force your bathroom habits outside of your house. You don't have that right.

It's unsanitary. And, let's face it. It's NASTY.

Except for the privacy of your home, here is a list of places where it is *uncool* to clip your nails. Ready?

Everywhere.

You should have done it before you left the house. They call it personal hygiene for a reason. Because your hygiene is your issue. But once you take it outside, you make it someone else's issue. Just because it's a public place, you simply can't do whatever you want. I'm here to tell you, no, no, you can't.

That's why you can't walk around with your pants *down* and your pookie showing. The public does not need—or want—to see it.

While you're cinching up your belt, think about this. Many states have laws against handheld electronics in cars, right? 'Cause it's dangerous. So why would it be any safer for folks to line their lips, put mascara on their lashes, clip their nose hair, or do any of the other things that we won't talk about . . . while they're behind the wheel at fifty miles per hour?

A lot of this is laziness. It's lazy people saying, "Oh, you know, I'll do it in the car." I say, No! No! No! No! No! Don't do it in the car. Do it at home. *Take the time*, get up *a little earlier*, and leave the house—*done*. So that when you get in the car, *you're driving*.

Which is what you're supposed to be doing.

Since we are on the subject, I don't want to smell you either. Good smell, bad smell, I don't want to spend the rest of my day trying to get your odor out of my hair and off my clothes. Perfume, BO, smelly feet, scented hand cream, *eau de cologne, eau de toilet*, none of it.

One of the reasons I wanted to write this book is because we are all getting crowded closer and closer together and we need to figure out how to make life pleasant for each other in spite of close proximity.

So as long as we're all crowded so close, let's deal with our smells . . . please??

We all try to be fresh for the day, which is fine. But God, how many times have you been stuck in a carpool with somebody day after day and they're wearing enough cologne to make your eyes bleed!!

And don't drop an air biscuit in the elevator. Need I say more? I think not.

Oh . . . And remember the windows in your car are made of glass. Stop picking your nose!

Let's face it. Hygiene is *so* important. If you know you haven't showered for a week or two—Yow!—your stink is pretty much going to be traveling with you. So maybe you might not want to get into a closed elevator. Unless you're an asshole. Because *assholes* will be stinky and get in the elevator with you.

But at least that elevator ride will be over eventually. Here's what's tough. What's tough is when you have to work all day around someone with bad hygiene. But, truth be told, you don't have to.

What's that, Whoopi, I don't?

No, you don't. If you work with someone who is chronically stinky, you can fix it. And the way to fix it is to tell them. They may not know. Why not sit them down and say, "You have an unusual smell. And I'm curious about it. Because I'm not sure if I can handle it or not." As opposed to being uncomfortable . . . on the brink of gagging every time the person comes around . . . and so what do you do? You stay away from them and they think you don't like them. And once you begin talking—and, dare I say, clear the air—in the long run, it becomes one less thing making your day bad.

I know, I know, some people feel uncomfortable about this. It's a tough line to cross 'cause it's so personal. But listen, it's only personal if they're home. If you're sharing a space with them every day at work, it is no longer a personal matter. You can ask that question. You don't need to do it in front of everybody. And, yes, *maybe* it will make them uncomfortable, but, you know what? Maybe it will actually help them.

The real question is to you.

If it's really a problem for you, ask yourself, how much do you want to change it? Can you *live* with it? Do you *want to*, or *have to*? And if they're a nice . . . albeit fragrant person . . . and somebody you'd like to be friends with, you're going to have to work this out. You're going to have to say something. Very gently and not in a bad way. Try something like, "Listen, this is really hard for me to ask you. But I have to because I really would like to have a better relationship or a friendship or spend some more time with you. But I have this question for you."

It's the only way. *Or live with it.*

Now. If this person is your boss, unless the job market looks good and you have an updated résumé . . . or perhaps, you hold a very promising lottery ticket . . . you may want to get real good at holding your breath. Your call.

It comes back to how bad do you want this to change? That's really the only question you have to ask yourself. If it's not worth it, don't do it. If it's worth it to you, and you can do it without being mean, I say go for it.

Where Is the Respect?

You should hear it inside my head. It's like a press conference in there . . . Question about this. Question about that. Question about why I asked myself that last question. But I think, for me, the biggest question in the world these days is, why don't people think before they act? I just dealt with this recently. The newspaper printed where I live. And it *really* pissed me off.

Why would they do it?

It's nutty. That's my home. Now, I'm sure those newspaper folks all have families. What if I just up and printed where their family lives? Where their kids go to school? Where they hide the key when they go away on vacation?

So, note to newspaper editor: How pathetic is it that my private information is the best news you can come up with?

What possesses somebody to print someone else's private information? When did an address become newsworthy? I haven't shot anybody, haven't killed anybody, I'm just on TV. I make movies. I make pizza. Does that make me less of a person on the planet?

NO!

(Thank you all for that response.)

Something like this could happen to anybody. It could be happening to you right now. Do you really believe you have to be famous to win the invasion-of-privacy lottery? Think again. Office gossip about subjects that used to be personal or intimate gets around in all sorts of ways now. Used to be they were just whispers around the water cooler. Or from toilet stall to toilet stall. Now they can end up with somebody putting it out there on their Facebook page or Twitter or in their emails.

Where the hell is the respect for one another?

And no, I'm not living a double standard. I know perfectly well that every day I am sitting amongst folks on a TV show that often can be intrusive of people's privacy. And yes . . . it drives me crazy.

It's a dilemma for me, and I'm conflicted. On the one hand, I have strong points of view on the subject of privacy, and on the other hand, there I am, talking to Jon and Kate . . . or whoever . . . sometimes about intimate aspects of their lives. So here's how I've decided to handle it. If there's something I want to ask, I'll ask it, but if I don't, I won't. Most times I don't. Because I don't want to know.

But I'm on a TV show that tells me that a lot of people do want to know. And often, people tell you everything anyway. It's mind-boggling. I'm good if you want to tell me what you're wearing. Or that you have two kids. Or you raise ducks. But sometimes, they just want to tell you stuff that's not your business. Maybe because they tweet or they're on FaceSpace, or whatever, and they're used to it.

And while I'm on the subject, some of them do reality shows where we see them drunk, or we see them with their seventy-eight kids, or we see them hanging out in their daily life. Oo, yippee!! That used to be a rarity, except for a documentary called *An American Family*, with the Loud family, which PBS ran back in the 1970s as one of the first reality shows. That was a huge deal. People just didn't share everything back then.

Now everyone does it. Because everyone thinks that they're fascinating. People used to say, "My life is a soap opera." Now everyone thinks their life would make a great reality show. It's now a life goal to aspire to be the next *Jersey Shore* dudebag or Reality Chick.

It seems like we are boundary-free. Folks blog now about what they ate for lunch. They're tweeting every time they stop for a latte, cross the street, or see a wad of gum stuck to a park bench that looks like Papa Smurf. People are walking around with camera crews! "That's my camera crew." ". . . What?! Your what? Why do you need a camera crew?"

Why are we so obsessed with pushing our lives out there to be lived in front of a camera? It's extraordinary.

If that's you, what is missing in your life that you need to fill that hole? So is the next step that's coming for all sorts of folks you don't even want to know prying into all your business? Business that you will suddenly decide is off limits. Like your address. Your diary. Who you're sleeping with. Or that you wore dirty sweats to the McDonald's and ate large fries, and with that belly on you.

Oops, silly me, it's too late. That genie's out of the bottle.

You Respect My Opinion, I'll Respect Yours

It used to be all right to disagree. It made life interesting. Now it draws blood. "End of discussion" can mean the end of a nice lunch. Or a friendship.

It's crazy. Can we turn that around? . . . Maybe.

A good starting place is cutting each other some slack. I hear people say, "Why do you always have to have an opinion?" Or "Why does that person always have to have something to say?" Well, maybe it's because they do have something to say. We have a choice, you know. We don't have to listen. We can leave the room.

We don't have to agree with it or like it, but it's their right to express themselves. Now, there are some things that are not OK to say. Like when you slander people? Not a good thing.

It's pretty simple. You want respect? You've got to give respect.

Respect my opinion, and I'll respect yours. If I want to offer you my opinion, you have two choices: You can listen, or not. And you can make that decision just like that.

Now. If you don't want to hurt my feelings by walking away, you can say, "You know what? I really don't want to talk about this. I'm not really interested in a deep airing of this subject." Or, screw it. You can walk away and let me deal with whatever the consequences are of expressing my opinion. And you know what? . . . If you let me deal with those consequences, I might start to realize that not everybody wants to hear it. So I might actually come to the conclusion myself.

We all have people in our lives who come from opposite sides of issues from us. When we get with these people, who we otherwise dearly love, some of them can't resist starting in . . . pushing all our buttons. It bugs us, but if we love them, we tolerate it. And, hopefully, move on in the conversation—the sooner the better.

Most of the time people just want a chance to speak. They want someone to know that they are thinking about this or that. Sometimes they don't get a lot of opportunity to talk about things in depth with folks. So they wait until they get around people they feel that they can get in deep with and say what's on their mind. And sometimes, it's just 'cause they want to hear themselves talk. Or they are desperate for contact. Even if what they're saying pisses me off. It's respect again. And because I know my patience is going to be tested when I see them, I do a self-talk beforehand so I can remind myself to be cool and maintain the respect. Doesn't always work, but I do try.

But the tone of things is definitely changing. You've seen it, I'm sure. Where it used to be, I disagree with you on this or that issue, now it's, "You're an asshole." Or "You're un-American."

And when things get heated up like that, bad things can happen. If you don't think so, let me remind you of a certain health care argument on a California sidewalk that grew into a street fight and someone got his finger bitten off. Now, I have been involved in some highly passionate discussions, but I can assure you that I have not once chomped off a finger . . . Wasn't even tempted.

When things get overheated and personal, nobody gets heard. Just hurt.

I think we can keep things civil. As one might say, "You could act that."

What happens when people get into attack mode is, instead of talking with each other, they talk at each other. There is a big difference. It's about give and take. Talking at somebody is different from talking with them because when you're talking with them, you actually *have to listen* to what they're saying. Then you respond. Or not. There's a back and forth that happens when you're talking *with* somebody. But when you're talking *at* somebody, you don't hear them. You're not listening. It's all about getting out your point. And that may be fine, but it doesn't move you forward. Because people glaze over when you talk at them—especially when you yell at them.

Now, to be clear, I'm talking about yelling at somebody. Not discussions that get passionate. There's a difference.

Most of the time, if you talk with people, and it stays a conversation—even if it gets passionate—you can move forward from it. It can even be fun. It's the difference between sparring and fighting. But the minute you shut down that two-way route, trouble is close by. Because then you are not challenging somebody, you're pretty much telling them they have no right to think, or speak, or feel what they're feeling.

I don't know when this started to change but, oftentimes, people do not listen at all. They hear what they want to hear. Or they only hear that one little thing you say that gives them permission to be angry at you, ignoring the rest.

Ka-boom.

On the other hand, some people are more open. I'm with someone on a constant basis whose mind changes a lot and says, "I've learned a lot of stuff." I'm talking specifically about my friend Elisabeth Hasselbeck. I don't know if she exactly says, "You've changed my mind," because I don't know if you can really change somebody's mind . . . but you can at least have a discussion. And they can look at it differently. And ponder that.

Elisabeth knows that, to me, it's a discussion. We get to talk and we get passionate. But it's never personal . . . which is why she will often be able to hear me and, maybe, say, "Oh, I hadn't thought about it from that perspective. Let me think about this and see how I feel about it." And that's why I love her.

Is it just me, or have we grown more cynical? Maybe with good reason, maybe not. But it still does not give us license to run amok over each other. Just because somebody calls you the Ugly American doesn't mean you get to go and be the Ugly American.

There were stories that, even though Ronald Reagan and Tip O'Neill were ideological foes, they still socialized. Those dudes would debate in the day, and at night, they'd hang. It used to be possible to have those head-butting things over issues and still be good friends. Used to be.

Maybe it still is. I got a glimmer of hope when I learned Senators Ted Kennedy and Orrin Hatch were such good pals. Think about it. If we only adapt ourselves to people who think exactly like we do—what's next? You have to look exactly like I do? You have to smell exactly like I do? How do you learn anything? Why wouldn't you want to hear a variety of opinions?

There are some basics we all agree on. Don't kill anybody. Don't yell "fire" in a crowded theater. Don't drop air biscuits in the elevator. There are some basics, yet there are still some problems in the way we relate to each other these days.

I even know of some people who won't date someone who they disagree with politically. Kinda dumb, but, hey, that's their choice. But what's the point?

This may surprise you, but I have a lot of friends who are staunch conservatives. Some don't believe in a woman's right to choose. Or in gay marriage. Or in interracial dating. In spite of those things, I still like them as friends. I don't understand or condone their beliefs, but some of those people are really funny or are deep thinkers. And I think sometimes it spices things up to have a little bit of healthy discussion. At least, I used to think so. But I listen to people now and it's, "Believe what I believe, or get out." A tad Taliban-esque, isn't it?

And more and more, it's, "Don't cross this line." But because I carry a spray can, I draw my own lines as I go.

How Not to Turn a Discussion into a Fight

- Don't call somebody stupid.
- Don't call somebody an idiot.
- Don't point and laugh.
- Don't repeat what the person just said in a cartoon voice.
- Don't roll your eyes and say, "Yuh, right," or "Duh."
- Don't freak when the other person gets passionate. Passion is not an attack.
- Don't personalize. Not in what you say. Not in what you hear. It's not about you. Don't make it about them. That is the path to ugly.
- Do take a full breath after the other person finishes a sentence before you start yours. Even a toddler will say to a parent, "I don't like it when you cover my words." So listen to some kid wisdom and leave space for the other person.

And smile once or twice. It'll keep things nice and civil. And if it doesn't, then it'll scare the crap out of the person you're talking to. Either way, you can't go wrong.

Daily Rehab

All right, so you screwed up. You had this big old argument, and in the heat of it, you said the wrong thing. And now somebody's got hurt feelings. And you did it. Are you going to do something to fix it, or not?

I wish I could help you, but I have never been in this position. My hands are clean.

I'm lying!

If someone comes to you and says, "You know what, you really hurt my feelings when you said, 'Blah-blah-blah . . .'"—you've got to respond to them. It's not hard. But focus. Because it's a huge deal to them. They need to hear you say, "I didn't mean to hurt your feelings. I'm really sorry. It doesn't change how I feel about the issue we were discussing, but what I said wasn't meant to hurt you." And that's all you can really do.

But again, let me reiterate: If you want to keep this person in your life, you've got to apologize, if that's what you feel (and if you don't feel it . . . at least look sincere).

If people care enough to tell you that you hurt their feelings, and you apologize—and, again, it is a genuine apology—you can move on. The question is, can the other person?

But I always caution, if somebody in your life hurts your feelings, ask yourself this. Is it something that happens a lot? Or often? Or is this just like a random, one time only, "Wow, I didn't know that was happening"? Look at it. See what it is. That should have a lot to do with how you respond to them.

If they're good people and happen to hurt your feelings for the first time, and they apologize, I say accept it. Heal up, laugh it off, and move on. If it happens every couple weeks, you two may need to have a bigger conversation.

And when you do your tallying, look at the numbers. See how often this happens, then ask yourself, is this a conversation I want to bother to have? How much do I want this to change? Or is this person a J-O-B job? Because if somebody's got a foot up your ass, and you're tired of it, it's probably best to let them know.

It's a good bet you can't move on until you do let them know.

And here's a shocker. Some people just don't want to move on. They either refuse your apology or else they say they accept it and then just keep acting like they're still pissed off at you. Maybe they still are. Or maybe they're one of those drama junkies who love the conflict more than the peace. You know them. They're the ones who get invited on the hayride and bring a book of matches.

Dealing with these people is painful. To work it out you may have to take yourself to some uncomfortable places emotionally. That's all fine. Chalk it up as part of the daily rehab we all do to keep moving forward in our lives. Whether it's worth it, though, is a question only you can answer.

But as long as you're asking yourself questions, ask this one. When somebody reaches out, what would you regret more, slapping the hand away, or accepting an apology so you can both move on?

Pretend it's you.

Even if the other person is at fault, these bad feelings are toxic in your life too. So you're also doing yourself a favor. Forgiveness works two ways when you put it out there.

But face it—some people just get stuck. Forgiveness isn't what they're all about. They're all about the anger. Their anger is their best friend and what would they ever do without it?

So if you've made a sincere attempt and it's refused, there's nothing you can do about that. At a certain point you've done all you can, and it's time for you to be moving on.

At least one of you should have a shot at being happy.

TSA Does Not Mean "Time to Smart Ass"

Flying is a chore. It is not glamorous. It's a day lost to aggravation and discomfort. And that's the good part. So what makes no sense to me is this: Why, oh why do people make it harder from the start by treating the airport security folks like crap? Look, we all get frustrated at having to stand in a long line. But we have to, so we do it. And what's our reward at the end of the ordeal? We get to take off half our clothes. Hoorah! But somebody tell me what it accomplishes to act out against the security agents.

Zip.

Don't these folks know that the TSA people are not there to mess with us? They're not there to make life difficult. The TSA people are there to make sure that we are all flying safe. So the annoyances . . . like you have to take your shoes off, or "I've got to go through your bag," or they've got to pat you down or swab the palms of your hands . . . that's them doing their jobs. So what good does it do to be nasty to the TSA person?

Let me see . . . I believe "zip" still applies.

I say, shock them. Don't be nasty, be cooperative. If you can, make them laugh. Because they are standing all day long with an endless parade of people who don't want to do what they have to do. And people who won't say, "You know, I think I'll take a Trail-ways bus instead." So if you have to go by air, you've got to do the drill at the airport.

Be ready for it. Have clean feet. Change your socks. Wash your feet. They may have to pat you down, so please make sure you're wearing deodorant! How's your breath? Check yourself before you go through the line. You've got enough time. Plane's probably late anyway. So just take your time and get organized. And don't take your frustration out by smart-assing the TSA people.

You know, they just don't need extra lip. They're getting nasty folks all day long. In their face. Sucking their teeth. Rolling their eyes . . . People who come with sixteen pounds of jewelry on. Why, God? Why do they do that when they know that you can't go through a metal detector wearing Tiffany's? So—one would think—that before they even got to the airport, they'd take the bling off and put it in a carry-on bag. Doesn't that make sense?

Yes. Yes, it does make sense.

And so does this: Don't pack your bag with things that you're not supposed to have. Because then everything has to *stop*. And why? So they can *go through your bag* and tell you what you should already know. So why set yourself up, and all the people waiting in that long, sad line behind you, for frustration?

It's so simple. If you're going to fly, prepare. Otherwise, get a private plane or Greyhound bus. But keep in mind, if you get on the bus, you've got to contend with that smelly toilet in the back. And, see, nobody cares if you roll your eyes on the bus, because they're all doing the same thing.

Remember, though, there is light at the end of the tunnel, and how much faster will it go if *you do not* put obstacles in your own way?

This is not Fantasyland. The rules are not going to change because you want them to. Or because you see yourself as an exception.

Sometimes somebody slips in line in front of you. Is it worth getting arrested over it? Is it really worth adding to the frustration of being on line by getting into a hassle with the bonehead next to you? Just because they're a bonehead doesn't mean you have to be.

Also, try and show up on time. If they tell you to arrive an hour and a half before, chances are you're going to be a lot calmer if you do. Now. There's all kinds of stuff that prevents that . . . things that slow you down. Number one, you've got traffic. That's understandable. But people, check your route. Have you got a radio? Have you heard of Traffic and Weather Together?

Some people don't want to leave their house two hours early—tough! If you don't want to be hassled, then give yourself enough time to get where you're going so you don't freak yourself out. What's the point of getting agitated?

Here's a simple math fact. Ready? If you left fifteen minutes late, you're going to be *fifteen minutes later* sitting in traffic. And it is not the other drivers' fault that you are in traffic and late. And driving fast isn't going to help. So make the decision. Leave two hours early. It's not the most fun, we all know that. But be early and sit at the frickin' airport. Bring a book, or a PSP, or a puzzle. At least once you are there, it's one less hassle to think about and you can relax and enjoy your trip.

But start it right. When you see that TSA agent, commit an act of kindness. Sometimes it's just a smile. And a "Thank you!" Because their job is tough. They are your first line of defense. So give them a break!

And let's all lighten up.

And while I'm on the subject of flying, remember . . . The airlines are not your friend. And they make great commercials that say they are.

It's a lie!

Smiley faces, friendly flight attendants patting your shoulder . . . passengers grinning 'n' gliding down the aisle to a clean 'n' comfy seat . . . food . . . That's just the pitch. They're just not your buddy. Airlines are there to make as much money as they can make, which is why you're not only still paying for checked bags on most of them, your pals are charging you even more than when they started. One airline wants to start charging for your carry-on bag too.

So the upshot of these friendly skies is what? Well, everybody's solution to the checked-bag fee is to carry on as much as humanly possible into that limited space aboard the plane.

You're only allowed to carry on two bags. One small suitcase that has to fit the bin and a shoulder bag or briefcase. So, if you're going on a trip, and if you don't have the dough to just pay to check all your bags, then you have to pack smarter.

What does packing smarter mean? It means that you're only taking what you need. Not what you think you're going to need, but what you really need. And if you don't want to spend the money to check luggage, please don't aggravate everybody else by being one of those Einsteins trying to sneak on extra bags. The truth of the matter is, if you do what they ask you to do and not try to be slick, there's space for everybody. Look around the boarding gate. Everybody else wants to be slick too . . . They also want to bring fifty-five bags on, but guess what? They can't. So please do what they're asking you to do.

Don't be a hog.

Now, if you're smart, and you don't want to spend that money, find out what it costs for UPS. I like to use FedEx or UPS to send bags ahead to my destination because I do not want to have all that with me on the plane. And I need larger bottles than are allowed by TSA for carry-on. So package them up and find out what it costs. The post office has great overnight and two-day service . . . and the chances of losing it are the same as the chances of losing it at the airport. So why not just go ahead and pack it up and call the destination that you're going to, whether it's a house or a hotel, and say you're sending it ahead? More and more people are doing this now, and the hotels pretty much have it all down.

It's also amazing what you can get away without. If you're going to Cancún, how much clothing do you actually need? Or if you're just going to go strolling, you bring your strolling clothes. But you don't need a fifty-pound suitcase to do that. If you're not going to the opera, chances are you can leave the tuxedo and the gown back home. Even if you do plan on dining out in nice restaurants a few nights, chances are, very few people in the population of the city you are visiting will remember what you had on the night before. So pack one outfit and get multiple uses out of it. Pack only for where you're going and for what you'll be doing. Everything else gets a stay-cation.

If you're going to a place that's really cold, like Colorado or New England in the dead of winter, chances are you should probably get one of those Space Bags, where you use the vacuum cleaner to suck the air out and shrink everything down. They work. They are really good products to have. If you've got a lot of clothing, pack it up, suck the air out, and put it in a suitcase. They work brilliantly on big woolly coats—they vacuum pack it. Think of it as an investment in your future!

Now, your stuff may be a little wrinkled, but that's what they make irons for. And every hotel has an iron and housekeeping! Call 'em. If you have a giant parka, you hang it up in the bathroom and turn on the shower so that it just moistens the air up, and poof! It's back, wrinkle-free.

I'm waiting for the day I can be vacuum-packed and mailed to my vacation destination. It's not exactly "Beam me up, Scotty," but it would mean no waiting in lines. The only bad part would be that my good friends at the airlines would be deprived of the fee for my carry-on. Know what? I can live with that.

How Not to Slow Down a TSA Screening

- Don't wear a ton of metal jewelry.
  Who are you trying to impress on the plane?

- Don't bring liquids.

- Know what you can't bring through.
  Go to www.tsa.gov.

- Be clean.
  These people have to deal with you in close quarters.

- Arrive early so you are not hassled going in.

- Don't shove or cut in line.

- If someone cuts the line on you, let it go.

- Hassle no one. Even if you are right.

- Pack so you don't have to dig for your computer.

- Have your ID ready. And the boarding pass.
  This is not new stuff.

- No jokes. No kidding.

- Take off your earphones. Be present.

- Get off the cell phone.

- Try and smile at the TSA folks.

- And say thank you.

Just Plane Good Manners

Is it me, or does annoying behavior seem worse when it happens on an airplane? Yeah, it does feel more annoying there. Because as uncomfortable, crowded, and emotionally draining situations go, flying . . . sitting all crammed together there in a pressurized tube for hours and hours . . . flying is right there on top of the list. If ever there was one place that good manners are appreciated and bad manners are noticed, it's on an airplane. Well . . . and maybe a submarine.

Crazy me. I thought we all had an obligation when we get on a plane to make sure that we don't create an uncomfortable situation for anyone else. How? Simple. Either because we drank too much . . . or don't want to comply with the rules of turning off the phone . . . or switching off the computer. Or just by being too loud and obnoxious. People have got to cut that out.

There are other people on that plane. And just like you don't want to be annoyed . . . they don't want to be annoyed either. So if everybody does what they're asked, chances are, it will be a really cool flight.

How easy is that?

People could start by lightening up on the flight attendants. You have to figure that crew has been dealing with other people before we got on their plane. Who knows? They might have just worked a red-eye cross-country with the drunk-on-their-butts cast from *Jersey Shore*. So, if they're not the cheeriest people you've seen all day, keep in mind you don't know what you're getting the wrath of. But again—a smile and a "How you doin'" can work wonders. Now, if they're just total crabs, you are allowed to say, "Come on, now, this is tough enough. So, hi, how are you?" That's OK to say. But you don't want to give the flight attendant too much crap. You don't want a big hassle.

Folks need to check their drinking on the plane. They just do. Six miles up in a jet is not someplace to get silly or drown sorrows. You're sitting in close proximity to other people so, come on, check that alcohol intake. Now, some people have to have a little sumpin'-sumpin' just to chill them out so they can fly. That's cool. But if you *know* that you can't do more than two drinks, *don't* have more than two. Don't do it. This is transportation, not *Mardi Gras*!

People who drink too much should be very aware that not only is it not cool for the flight attendants, but it's not cool for the rest of the people on the plane. On the ground, drunks make everyone tense. In the air . . . they freak everyone out. Nobody knows what the hell a drunk's going to do. And most drunks, you can't reason with them. There is no logical discussion with someone who has altered their state. So if you want to get hammered, keep in mind that your behavior on that plane may not bode well for you when you land. Because, here you thought you were going on vacation, and instead, you're going to jail. Why? Because you knew that you shouldn't have had that fourth drink. And you *knew*!

These days, you can't fool around. You just can't. So why, with everybody paranoid about terrorists and nut jobs . . . why would you want to make other people on the plane nervous that you're going to do something unpredictable? And if you're an alcoholic, here's what I want to say to you. You need to substitute some hard thinking for the hard drinking.

Hey, they should maybe put that on a cocktail napkin.

It is scary, though. And if you're traveling with someone who you know is a belligerent drunk, let somebody else know. Get up. Talk to the flight attendant. If you don't want the drinker to know that's what you're doing, walk to the back bathroom where they can't see you doing it. Grab a flight attendant and say, "Listen, this person drinks a lot. And if you give them more than this, they can be a hassle." Alert people so you can get some help—so, A, you're not handling this all by yourself, and B, you're taking into consideration other people on the plane. And if you can do that, most flights would be all right.

Even better when the pilots pass the Breathalyzer.

Oh. Delicate subject, but we're among friends, right? If you've been a little sickly, or your stomach has been acting up, follow the rules of "If I Was Walking in after Me . . ." So, if it's possible, in your handbag or in your back pocket, bring a little freshener thing that can ease the scent in the can. Take your little Magic Tree and hang it up in there. Do something nice. That's not a bad thing.

And after you use the head, clean up, please. Don't leave water and soap suds all over. Again, other people are sharing the space. You know when you've made a mess. Don't leave it for somebody else. You'd be mad as hell if you came into that bathroom and it was a wreck. So, you know, show a little thought for the people who are on the plane with you. Wash your face, sure. But if you make a mess around the sink, clean it up. It takes no time.

Also, if you happen to see that the toilet paper has like four sheets left, let the flight attendant know. Because nobody wants to walk in there and sit down and look over and see there's no toilet paper. There's no reason for it. Also, keep in mind everyone knows it's you—there are only three bathrooms, and these days we now watch anyone who gets up, so pretend you're going to be the next one in.

Pretend it's you.

All this stuff is fresh on my mind because I started flying again last year. My fear of flying came from seeing two planes collide. That, you know, cannot happen again. Not unless someone is trying to ram you with their airplane. There are stopgaps put into place that will keep that from being an issue again. High five for technology!

I took the step to get over my fear after I got whorish and accepted a job in London and they were sending a private plane for me. Gulp. But know what? Because I talked about my fear of flying, the people at Virgin said, "Wait a minute, we have a program that might help."

It's an amazing course for folks who won't, or can't, fly. The Virgin people put me with a pilot and a psychologist, plus someone who had successfully been through the program. And so I sat with them for five hours the day before I was getting on the private plane. I felt better because I learned that a lot of the things that were keeping me back don't exist anymore. When we finished, I said to them, "OK, I hear and see everything you've shown me and I feel like if I can do this thing to London, and if I feel the same when I come back, I will take myself to the airport, get on a plane, and go to LA and knock on my daughter's door."

And that's what I did.

Now, I still hate flying. It's not something I want to do. But now it's something I *can* do.

So here I am. Now I can fly again and be up there cruising along at thirty-five thousand feet. With all the drunks, and the bin hogs, and the guy with the dirty hands trimming his fingernails on the seatback tray.

Lucky me.

Even Steve Jobs Has to Turn Off His Cell Phone

I have been called a lot of things. But compliant is not often one of them. Some might even say, "She's compliance-challenged." Or "compliance-unfriendly." Yes, I'm the one who colors outside the lines and in the boldest colors I can find. My drum does beat a little differently. But, hey, you get me on an airplane, and I am the Borg from *Star Trek*. I assimilate. That is to say, I become a compliance freak.

They keep the rules pretty simple. Buckle the belt. No gathering in the aisles, especially not by the cockpit door. No smoking. No assaulting crew members. And turn your electronics off when they tell you to.

Not too challenging, right?

Then why, oh, why do so many folks have trouble powering down their electronics? Some people kind of forget. I guess they're too busy figuring out how to recline their seatback into the bridge of your nose. But there are some people who try to be slick. They palm their cell phones or hide their computers when the flight attendants are near.

What's slick about that? Hey, Mr. Slick . . . know what your computer is actively doing when it's on in that critical time of takeoff and landing? It is interfering with the safety of all the other passengers. That's why they are really adamant about your turning off your computer until you're up and running.

What's the point? They didn't see you leave it on. Aren't you something. You got over this time. But what happens if something goes wrong, and it's your computer's fault because it's not in the mode it's supposed to be in? Which is off.

Again. All everyone has to do are the few things they need to do. It's easy. And it's common sense. If everybody's computer is off, then there's not an issue. Simple! You cannot be playing with your computer. Just turn it off.

It's fifteen or twenty minutes. Are you seriously going to say you can't deal with that?

Most people reading this are thinking the same thing right now. It's the same thing the passengers around you are thinking: Is your life so much more important than everybody else's? Are you too big to turn your computer off? No. Even on a private plane they ask you to do the same thing. Turn it off until they get up and running. It's a safety issue there's no reason to mess with.

If you have an iPhone, or another cell phone model that has an airplane mode, everybody knows they can click it to that, and still listen to their music, or play their games, or do whatever they want to do during the flight. But you can't do phone calls. So why would you? Do you really want to fool with the navigation equipment on the plane? You want a safe flight, the pilots want a safe flight. These are the things we all need to comply with in order to have a safe, easy flight. Why not just do it?

If you're one of those who tries to sneak text messages and cell phone calls in-flight, let me ask you this: What makes you more important than everyone else on the plane? They want to talk to their loved ones, make business calls, and text too. So who do you think you are? Because, pretty much, if they catch you, they're going to take it and you won't get it back until you land. And maybe not even then. They may have to take it in and see what you were doing with it. Were you trying to make something bad happen to that flight? So you are opening yourself up to so many unnecessary hassles.

All just so you can say to somebody, "Guess where I am? On the plane!"

And then it's like, "OK . . . and?" In case you hadn't noticed, a lot of folks are flying these days, so the person you're calling is probably not especially impressed. What are you doing that can't wait? Why take the chance of being in an uncool position for three hours when you can avoid it by just turning it all off?

Even Steve Jobs has to turn his phone off. The pope has to turn his phone off. Obama has to turn his phone off . . . You are no better than anybody else on that plane. Regardless of what you think. And you are surrounded by the same rules and obligations.

So follow 'em!

A Traveler Check

*Do you help other passengers with their overhead luggage when
they need a hand?*
    If yes, score 0
    If no, score 2

*Have you ever gotten drunk on a flight to the point the flight
attendant said you were cut off?*
    If no, score 0
    If yes, score 5

*Have you ever been reprimanded by a flight attendant for
your behavior?*
    If no, score 0
    If yes, score 5
    If more than once, score 10

Did it bother you?
    If yes, score 2
    If no, score 5

*Do you make it a point to clean up your mess before you
leave the restroom?*
    If yes, score 0
    If no, score 5

Have you ever used your computer or cell phone when
it's not allowed?

> If no, score 0
>
> If yes, score 5
>
> If regularly, score 10

When it's time to get off the plane, do you wait for rows to clear
in order, or do you squeeze ahead of the crowd?

> If you wait, score 0
>
> If you squeeze ahead, score 5

Total score: _____

Tally your score and write it in on the Master Score Sheet
at the back of this book, page 195.

Fragrant Fliers

A lot of airlines don't serve food anymore. Count your blessings. Those that do charge you five hundred dollars for a snack bag you can't get open. And when you do, your reward is three mini pretzels.

That's the good news—three pretzels. But the bad news is that most people are bringing on their own food.

Yikes.

Has anyone noticed the . . . unusual fragrances . . . on airplanes now? I suggest . . . have a little sense when you bring food aboard a plane. Because you're in a little closed cabin, and you don't want to be testing everybody's gag reflex. Come on, people. Wait the four freakin' hours to get where you're going to have stinky cheese. Bring yourself some crackers and some jelly or apple butter. How about one of those energy bars just to fend off the hunger pangs until you land? Bring something that isn't going to stiffen other people's nostrils or send them into anaphylactic shock.

Some people crack open that Tupperware and you can see the heads just starting to turn this way and that. Noses go in the air, faces start wincing. Know what that look is? That's the "WTF?" look.

Is that the look you want to be getting? Then don't pack along anything that's really pungent—overpowering foods that you might be used to but other people might not be. And hope to never smell again.

Once their sense of smell returns . . . if it ever does.

I mean, come on. Some of that grub smells so foul I expect to see the oxygen masks drop.

Look, it's not going to mess you up not to have the stinky fish for four or five hours, is it? Or an overabundance of garlic. Unless you plan on encountering a vampire in-flight, I'll bet you can survive without the garlic.

Your best solution is just to eat a little something before you get on the plane. But if you have a long flight and need a snack, what about bringing something like cut-up veggies—some carrots and celery—and maybe some hummus? They make a packaged hummus and pretzels that will keep your stomach from growling.

Keep it simple. That way you get something in your tummy . . . Plus that way, you won't have to see all those heads craning over the seat backs at you . . . trying to figure out who's the jerk eating the roasted whole cod in garlic sauce.

Stinky Foods Not to Bring on a Plane

- Cabbage-based anything. Coleslaw, sauerkraut.
- Tuna fish salad, even in a sandwich. Any fish. Any. Fish.
- Including gefilte fish. It may not look like a fish, but it sure smells like one.
- Lox (it's fish, right?)
- Anything with garlic
- Chili
- Chili dogs
- Chili fries (if your airport sells them, eat them before you board)
- Strong cheeses. Where do you think the term "Cut the cheese" comes from?
- Liverwurst
- Sausage and peppers subs
- Kielbasa (I'm calling you out, Chicago)
- Pizza with onions. Do I need to mention anchovies?
- Egg salad
- Hard-boiled eggs. Yup, that's exactly what they smell like.
- Cheeseburgers with onions
- Onions appear to be a theme
- Kim chi
- Caesar salad
- If it's in Tupperware with a spicy sauce, come on. Especially Indian food with a curry, or some Mexican dishes. Why tempt fate?
- French fries. Nothing like a whiff o' grease from your fellow traveler.

. . .

A few words about nuts and peanuts:

People with severe nut and peanut allergies can have a really bad day if someone's eating them nearby. Sometimes the crew will make an announcement if such a person is aboard. If so, be nice. Be a squirrel. Store your nuts until you land.

As long as we're on the subject of being kind to the noses of others, let's remember that your workplace might be a closed space, too. So in addition to the foods on our airplane list, here's another one that will help you make friends on the ground:

FUNKY FOODS NOT TO MICROWAVE IN THE OFFICE

Many workplaces no longer give employees a full lunch break. Or maybe you are doing your best to save some money and bring a lunch. You need to know that the microwave in the break room broadcasts the odor of your lunch. Notice I didn't say aroma. An aroma is what it smells like to you. To everyone else, it's an odor.

Avoid these odiferous microwave no-no's:

- Popcorn. Yes, popcorn. Ask anybody. It stinks.
  And hangs there all day.
- Broccoli or cauliflower
- Soups with broccoli or cauliflower
- Onion soup
- Certain prepared meals, especially diet meals,
  are lethal.
- Last night's Mexican combo plate
- Last night's chicken tikka masala

- Lamb kabobs or lamb stew
- Exotic foods of the world will not make you a goodwill ambassador.
- Anything with vinegar. Phew.

There's plenty other good stuff to eat. Unless you really enjoy getting the "WTF?" look as you walk back to your desk.

Babes on a Plane

We all know there is no airline just for parents, OK? So when small kids need to fly, the question needs to be asked, how do we do this together? My feeling is this . . . We've got to try to give as much help as we can to the person who's got the baby. Especially if you are the one stuck next to them. Love it or hate it . . . you will be stuck for hours—so help them out. They don't want a screaming baby either. They don't want the baby to do what it's doing. But a baby's going to do what babies do. And what do they do? They scream.

If you're in a seat next to a screaming baby, you have two choices. You can simply turn to the person who's got the kid and say, "What can I do to help you?" Or, you can say, "Is it really going to be that bad if you give the child what it wants?" Because for the five hours you're going to be on this plane, the baby's going to be really unhappy because it wants the keys, or the ring, or whatever.

Baby wants the toys.

The thing about babies on planes is that it's not an "if." No, it's more like a "when" the screaming's going to happen. But chances are, if you're the parent, you kind of know what's going to piss 'em off, and what's not going to piss 'em off. Babies want to get down and walk around. They can't. It's not possible. Babies cannot walk up and down the aisles. So it helps to bring enough stuff along that keeps them occupied. As the parent, it is your responsibility to keep the baby entertained. Trust me, I know you want to sit back and close your eyes—even for just one glorious minute . . . God, what we would all give for just that one minute—but if you're not traveling with someone else, you can't.

If you are the lucky seatmate, earplugs may dampen all the sound, but if that baby is trying to roll out of the seat and get away from the mother and do all kinds of baby stuff, earplugs don't mean squat. So do you want to make this work? Then I'd take out the earplugs and the first thing I'd say is, "What can I do to help you?" . . . By the way, you do know I mean to say that to the parent, right? You can say it to the baby if you want, but don't expect much of an answer.

So-called "experienced parents" like to give advice to folks traveling for the first time on an airplane with a baby. Useless tips like "It's important to remember that you'll never see any of those people again."

That only works for about five minutes. Because for the five hours that you're with them, they are boring a hole into your head. Your skull is about to give like a Gulf oil leak . . . because your baby is just performing. And in airplanes, what do they have? A built-in audience that can't move. For hours. So just get everything together. Have the bottle someplace where you can keep it handy. Have the baby toys that you know you will need.

Like I said, there's no Parent Air, which is what I would start if I were going to start an airline. It's a great idea and, if the right person is reading this book, we could start Parent Air.

In the meantime, I wish that the airlines provided baby things to play with. They could, maybe, give out little mobiles and things like that. Or those special crayons for little kids. Yeah, that'll happen. Sure it will. The same day they stop charging for bags and the pilots come around to give in-flight neck rubs. So, in the meantime, just be prepared that it's all on you and that your focus for the next five hours is going to be on the baby.

Oh, another thing . . . I know I may be piling on here, but this one is very important, OK?

If you're a parent of a child who is going to—perhaps—act up, don't pretend you don't see it. Or hear it. Or that you don't know that it's freaking people out. Acknowledge it. And, at least, give the folks around you the look that says, "I don't know what to do." But don't act like it's not happening. Because that pisses people off even more. Don't ignore it. And just because you're allowed to fly with your baby, doesn't give you the right not to care that other people who may not have children are going to be on there too. And they may not dig it. In fact, they may be very uncomfortable with it. And a "deal with it" attitude from you doesn't really go far in making friends or having people like your baby. So let them see that you're actively trying to do everything that you can do. Who knows, you may even win over some folks and get some help you didn't expect.

It's not an easy feat to take babies with you when you're going somewhere, because they get crabby, they want stuff, and they want to be B-U-S-Y.

That's why it's not a bad idea to start practicing with the kid before you travel. Sit for ten minutes just holding on to the baby so they get used to it. Otherwise, it's a new experience all around, and they won't like it. And will they ever let you know. So just start doing little things that you know you're going to have to do on the plane. Figure out ways to make it work, because you will be surrounded by other people who are trying to get through their nightmare too.

And, once again, a smile goes a very long way. It may not help, but it goes a very long way.

What to Bring for a Kid on a Plane

If you are a parent experienced in flying with children, turn the page. But plenty of new moms and dads haven't yet been exposed to the joys of travel with kids. For you, here are some tips on what to bring along to make your trip better:

- Storybooks and coloring books. DO NOT forget the crayons.
- A *silent* electronic toy or game like a PSP
- Plastic keys
- Make a little photo album of friends and family to flip through.
- An MP3 player with headphones and kid music
- That special stuffed teddy bear or whatever makes your child feel relaxed
- Bring the Blankie. But be careful. Don't forget it and leave it on the plane. It happens. Ask any shrink. I still fly with my Blankie.

The TSA does let you bring along formula, breast milk, medications, and baby food in reasonable sizes over the 3.4 ounce limit. They just want you to declare it to the agent when you get to the checkpoint. The rules change, though, so if you're not sure, contact the airline or look on the TSA website: www.tsa.gov.

Louder, They Can't Hear You in the Lobby

Is it just me, or do people simply not recognize they are out in public? They seem to think they're in their living rooms. Am I alone here? I think not.

If you are also getting irritated by this more and more and don't know how to address the problem—and by "problem" I mean "those loud people who think they are home"—I may be able to help. I shall now address them on behalf of all of us:

The theater is not your living room.
(I'm counting movie theaters, Broadway theaters . . . theaters in the park).

I repeat:

It's not your living room.

It's simple.

If it's that hard not to talk for two hours, maybe you ought to keep your ass home!

Here's the point. *Everybody* has paid their $75,000 to get into the movie, and they want to watch it, or see the show. So why do you feel the need to pretend like you're sitting in your living room having a conversation with your husband?

What gives anyone the nerve to step on my right to enjoy myself in silence? If you want to talk through it—go home! And why, in the movies, are you surprised when suddenly the usher comes up and goes, "'Scuse me. You are talking way too much." Now everybody is distracted. Congratulations, you have created an issue where there didn't have to be one. You've brought attention where you didn't have to have it. You've disrupted everybody's good time. All you had to do was know where you are . . . which is NOT at home!

THE MOVIES

Now. There are cultural differences that exist when you go to certain movies. Sometimes when you go to the movies in, say, a black neighborhood, folks talk to the screen. Know that. That's part of the show. I don't know why. It's what happens sometimes. White neighborhoods don't seem to talk to the screen. Unless it's *Rocky Horror*.

But if you're in the theater, and you're the only one making noise . . . there's a problem. If you can hear yourself in the movies . . . there's a problem. Can you guess what it is? Run to the mirror. What do you see?

You. Yes, you.

Imagine a movie *you* want to see, that *you* were enthralled by, and you've got some bonehead giving you play-by-play or asking about the Sno-Caps. Or talking about the fact that you don't think that actress is all that great . . . or that she's any good in this movie. Who wants to hear it? You don't want to hear that. You're shushing people when you're watching TV at home, so why do you think it's OK to go to the movies and act out? Have a little consideration for your neighbors who are sitting around you. Staring laser beams at the back of your head.

Because if *everybody* starts to exhibit that kind of behavior, you've got all kinds of problems.

So remember. Know where you are. And if you're in a movie where everybody is talking, knock yourself out. But if you are not, then—how can I put this nicely?—shut up!

Oh, and don't bring little kids to the movies. You know what I mean. I mean the movies that are not meant for little kids. I understand sometimes you don't have any money to get a babysitter and you just really want to go to the movies. OK. *Go in the morning.* Go to the ten a.m. show. Don't go to the eight p.m. show. *Because* you *know* babies are going to be cranky. Or it's going to be too loud for them. Or too scary for them.

So if you find yourself desperate to get out of the house and go to the movies, go early, because you *know* you're going to have to get up and leave because the baby doesn't want to be there anyway in the dark, just sitting there. Kids don't sit still. And their attention span is relatively short. So they psych you out for like, twenty minutes, and then they go off.

Who's enjoying the movie now? You? The baby? . . . Nobody!

And think about that child. Some kids have issues, like being sound sensitive. You need to know that before you take them into the THX theater. That big low rumble that sounds so great to *us* when the mother ship is landing may not sound all that great to a kid. And they can't explain it. They may not have the words yet, so they do the next best thing. Flip out.

And little kids will talk through a movie. "What *is* that?" "Why is he doing that?" "When is this going to be over?" "Can we go?" "I have to go to the bathroom." "Could I have something to eat?"

So if it's not the best experience for you, for the kid, or for the people in the theater with you, doesn't it seem like a lot of trouble for a $25 soda?

THE STAGE THEATER

As a performer on the live stage, one thing that irritates me is people coming in late. Yeah, traffic can be a factor, anything can happen, fine, fine, fine . . . But coming in after a show has started distracts everyone—folks acting and folks watching. 'Cause now, all we see is you . . . late . . . making noise (I really do hope it's not you who ends up getting those ugly stares). So avoid being late, if you can.

Ringing cell phones are also a pain. Folks let them ring and ring because they are hoping and praying nobody will figure out it is theirs.

Sorry, but everybody knows it's you. They *know* it's you. The people sitting around you are looking dead *at you*, saying silently, "This jackass's phone has gone off. And look, he's not doing anything." If you're at a play, or you're at a performance, those people on the stage can hear your phone. So just fumbleflub around and turn it off. Just do that. Best thing is just to turn it off as soon as you sit down.

The only person who should have any kind of device that goes off in a theater is a doctor. They're the only people that *have to* have their cell phones with them.

Here's another pain in the ass new technology has brought us . . . People in the theater audience have started to shoot video on their phones. You have to know it's a lousy thing to do. It's piracy. It's one of the things that irritates the hell out of me. 'Cause, basically, you are *stealing* somebody's performance.

Why do you think that's OK?

When I'm on a stage by myself, I say, "You cannot have your cell phone on. And if I see it, I'm going to put you out of here." People get offended! They tell me they paid their money. I say, "Hey, you paid your money to come to the theater, that's true, but I don't remember a DVD giveaway included, so turn it off or get out, because you haven't paid me for that."

It's rude, I know, but so is stealing my work.

And I feel bad for people in the audience who just wanted to see a show and now what do they have to do? They have to crane their necks to look around the guy holding up his cell phone to video it.

Am I the first one to wonder when a nice night in the theater stopped being just a night in the theater?

This cell phone recording is why so many comics and solo performers have changed the way they do things now. For instance, there's a whole lot of stuff now that I just won't say. I won't say it because I don't want my performance on YouTube out of context. And I can't even find you. It's anonymous. And that's cowardly. You can edit it, you can cut it, you can do whatever you want to it and take my work someplace maybe I wasn't going with it. But no one else knows that because they weren't there.

Anyone give you the right to do that? Just because you have the technical capacity doesn't mean you have the right to. Any more than it gives you the right to cut a hole in somebody's wall and videotape them changing their clothes. What is the moral obligation of technical access? Is there one?

Does your cell phone make you so important you are emboldened to do whatever you want with it . . . wherever and whenever you want to? Texting? Talking? Videoing?

I say, if you're that important, stay home. If you need to catch every beep and buzz that your phone does, stay home. Rent one of my DVDs and make us both happy.

EVERYWHERE ELSE

By now, if you go out you should know that there are certain things that are not OK. You don't have the right to stick your phone in somebody's face, you don't have the right to make me listen to your conversation. You're not entitled to that.

Whisper if you have to answer the phone in public. Be considerate. Because the little bit of space that I occupy in that restaurant is mine.

Now, why have I gone off this way? Because—to put it delicately—our manners have gone in the freakin' toilet. Dainty, aren't I?

I don't know if bad cell phone manners can be stopped. I truly don't. I believe cell phone rudeness is spreading in such a way that we are becoming a society where it doesn't even matter what the law says. If your state has a hands-free cell phone law, ask yourself how many people you see still holding the wheel with one hand while they talk. And that's only because the other hand is holding a sandwich! People still text while driving because they think they know how to do it. That's nuts. They forget there are fifty billion other people on the road who may be thinking the same thing and who also assume the laws of the land, not to mention the laws of Nature, don't apply to them either.

WTF?!

Even out of the car, cell phones are still a nuisance. But if you are a rude cell phone user, do you even know it? No, there you are, out in public with us folks just trying to go about our day, and you don't think to turn the thing off. OK, maybe you forget. Or maybe you don't care. But it goes off, and, instead of *getting up* and stepping out of the restaurant, or just turning it off, or seeing who it is and saying, "I'll call you back," you sit there and have a conversation, which I don't need to hear! I don't want to hear, really.

I don't want to hear it when you're going down the street, I don't want to hear it when you're in the elevator, I don't want to hear it when you're in a restaurant. Keep. That. To. Your. Self.

But you don't. Why? Because, like most people . . . when they get on their cell phones . . . they shout, like suddenly they're deaf and have no concept that they're sitting around other people. It doesn't matter to them. Because they *have* to talk on the phone.

"NO, THIS IS A GREAT TIME TO TALK ABOUT THE NEW DRAPES. WANNA HEAR?" No. As a matter of fact, I don't. But let me ask . . . Since when did my rights get usurped by your need to talk to your decorator? . . . In my face?

And here's the irony. If you challenge these boneheads, they'll turn to you and say, "Hey this is a private conversation, buddy."

"Well, actually, no. I can tell you what you said, I can tell you what you did, and, by the bye, I don't think you should make that move with those window treatments." Even if you are trying not to listen, you don't have a choice.

Oh, and how about this one? Sometimes cell phone rudies treat you to music! Wonderful! What a boon to us music lovers to sit there and listen to someone audition their ring tones, trying to decide which one to use. "Hm, is my girlfriend a Katy Perry or more of a Rihanna? . . . Or maybe the *Jaws* theme?" And they don't even know they're doing it. People act like there's an actual Cone of Silence that comes down over them. I'm here to tell you, no Cone, kids. I can actually hear you. I can see what you're doing, I hear everything you're saying.

So what can you do?

Well . . . you can hope people read this book that you're reading. There's an idea. Give them a copy of the book. And then go buy another one for yourself. Or call the bookstore and order one.

Just don't do it on your cell phone when you're in a restaurant sitting next to me.

Places Not to Use a Cell Phone

Unless you are a doctor, turn the cell phone off or don't use it when you are:

- In the movies

- At a play

- In a restaurant

- On a train. Move to the vestibule.

- Driving, unless hands-free. And even then . . .

- In church

- At parents' night in your kid's classroom

- In the elevator

- In a meeting at work

- During a family dinner

- At the cash register while someone waits on you

- In line. Any line. Nobody wants to hear it.

- On a hotel or apartment balcony

- During sex. Unless it's phone sex.

Thank You for Not Texting

I don't have an answering machine. I'm not there? Call me back. I turn my phone off after a certain time for a simple reason. I want that time to myself.

I see so many people with their BlackBerrys, and they can be reached 24/7.

Not for me.

Is it for you? Hm . . . say . . . you're not addicted or anything, are you? Good.

Just to be sure, let me ask you a couple of questions: Do you take your BlackBerry into the bathroom? Do you reach for it first thing when you wake up? Can you put it down? Have you forgotten how to have conversations over dinner without your BlackBerry? Do you reach for it the moment it pings? You do? Huh . . . Have you wondered what is going on in your life that you can't leave that message to sit there without having to respond instantly? Isn't that kinda like . . . an *addiction*??

Seriously. Do you really want to be reached in the shower? In the bathroom? Every second that you're awake, do you want someone to be able to put their hands on you? Where is your time alone? Do you get any? Most people that have BlackBerrys do not. They don't have alone time. They don't know how to do it anymore. They can't resist the textation.

Try this. Take the time to leave the BlackBerry outside of the bathroom door when you're home. And see what happens.

Put it down. Leave it upstairs. Leave it somewhere and see how you do. See if you can do without being connected twenty-four hours a day—if you're not a doctor.

Just try turning it off for one evening. And then turn it back on the next morning . . . and guess what? You didn't really miss anything . . . except someone's annoyed at you because they wanted you when they wanted you. Well, it's not about them. It's about you. And reclaiming your life by being a person that says, "Here are my work hours . . . This is when I can be reached."

People don't really have an actual vacation now because they have their BlackBerrys with them 24/7. Now, before The Digital Rage, people would go away for two weeks and wouldn't check in at the office. Now some folks say, "Well, I can do both and stay away longer," but, come on, most people can't. You not only don't stay away longer, you can't really call it time off . . . can you? Try this next time you take your kids on vacation—and you should take your kids on vacation. Don't check your BlackBerry every five minutes. Otherwise, you might as well be home.

It's hard. They call it a crackberry for a reason. And guess what? If you are a crackberry addict and want to kick the habit, you have to do it yourself. And a good place to start is by telling people that's what you're doing. Don't worry, you don't have to stand up in front of a room and say, "My name is so-and-so, and I am a crackberry addict," or anything like that . . . although, I bet that's coming. What you do have to do is set boundaries with people. You've got to say to them, "Between these hours, I'm not taking calls except from my kids. Unless it's an emergency, I don't need to be this connected."

I think this is one of those generation things. You know, another place where age clashes with youth. Because when you are of a certain age you can say, "You know what? I'm turning all this off, I've had enough for one day," and you do. But young people live on a twenty-four-hour cycle. They don't know about respites.

Also, people have to realize that when they set an example of spending their lives on call . . . having their BlackBerry out of their pocket, checking it all the time . . . they can't be shocked when they take the family to dinner—and *everybody's* got their BlackBerry out! It's the family meal, and every one of them has their heads bowed. And, as much as it looks touching . . . like a Norman Rockwell painting of a family saying grace . . . they aren't. They're all looking under the table, texting!!

My grandkids do it all the time. Because they don't know what it's like not to be able to reach somebody for one full hour. Or, maybe, ten minutes.

Once upon a time, we lived in an era where you had to *wait* to get home to get on the phone and tell somebody something. Or you had to have enough change in your pocket. When did 9 to 5 suddenly turn into 24/7? Would you have thought to call someone at the restaurant where they were eating? Or at the dentist? That's the next step. Dentists are going to have to work around patients reclining in the chair holding their BlackBerrys up over their heads, tapping away on their little keyboards.

"OMG, I am so slobbering right now."

Would you have thought to call someone at the . . . casino table? No. When you got back to your room, you saw that you had messages. And you responded when you were ready. But now, how long can you be away from it? Not long, otherwise, it's like, "Where the hell were you?"

Personally, I think it could be healthy to let people know it's none of their business. Tell them they don't need to know everything you're doing every second of your life. Say you were sitting in the park. "Why couldn't I reach you?" "Because I didn't pick up my phone! Because I didn't want to be bothered at that moment." "But I needed to talk to you." "OK, what is it? Huh? What did you want to talk to me about?" "I just wanted to know if you were going to this thing." "And you couldn't wait to find that out? No one died, no one got into an accident? You just wanted information— when *you* wanted it."

We've become a society that wants instant response. So we cannot be thoughtful. We cannot think about what our response is going to be because—*ping*! People are waiting for us to respond to them immediately.

I think one of the reasons people are freaking out so much these days is because the pressure that they would have had to deal with before they got connected has now quadrupled. They call it "wired" for a reason, you know? Because now, it's like, BUZZ-BUZZ-BUZZ, I'm calling you. Or, PING-PING-PING, I'm Black-Berrying you. OK, so, I've looked at your message, and, know something? To me . . . I don't need to answer you immediately.

But they want an answer immediately.

Because that's what *they* need. Now. How do we work it out? I freak myself out by staying on those things. So, yeah, busted . . . true confession time . . . Recently I've been dealing with it too. Every time it buzzes, I'm all, "Who wants me? Who's talking to me?" There's something inherently wrong with that. Because you lose so much of your personal time and freedom that it's scary.

Don't get me wrong, there are great reasons to be connected. If you're in a car and something's gone wrong, you got a flat tire, or you've got to call the police, or whatever. You've got to get hold of your mom . . . that's all great. But this idea that you cannot have a moment's peace without being constantly found is insane to me.

You were just checking your BlackBerry, weren't you?

What the hell!

Resisting Textation

How often do you check for incoming texts and emails?
    If several times a day, score 0
    If hourly, score 1
    If every ten minutes, score 5
    If you monitor constantly, score 10

Has your spouse or your child ever asked you to put your handheld device aside for once?
    If no, score 0
    If yes, score 5

Has anyone ever taken your handheld out of your hands to get your full attention?
    If no, score 0
    If yes, score 5

Did you ignore it and pay attention to them?
    If yes, score 1
    If no, score 2

Do you sneak texting in meetings at work or at social events or dinner?
    If no, score 0
    If yes, score 5

Have you ever gone one night without emails or texts?
    If yes, score 0
    If no, score 5

If you are alone reading a good book and you hear your incoming email or text sound across the room, what do you do?

If you finish your chapter and then check, score 0

If you cross immediately to see what it is, score 5

Total score: _____

Tally your score and write it in on the Master Score Sheet
at the back of this book, Page 195.

A Flea on the Ass
of a Mosquito

Have you been to a sporting event recently at a stadium or arena? Is it just me, or has the language in the stands gotten ruder and cruder?

First of all, anyone calling out obscenities at a sporting event is really not acting smart. Especially if you are someone who has children along. A lot of people . . . people with their kids right there at the game with them . . . yell out really rude stuff. And then they're shocked when their kids do the same thing. And other people have their kids there too. It makes no sense to me.

Unless you are me—up on a stage—nobody wants to hear somebody cussing up a storm about whatever's bugging them. And the difference is this . . . when someone hears me do it, they knew that was part of the show when they bought the ticket. I'm a performer, not some heckler from the bleachers popping off a mouthful of ugliness in front of children. And you know you're going to find children at sporting events—unless it's your penitentiary softball game . . . in which case, have at it!

Imagine if we all lost our minds for a day and just started heckling each other the way that we heckle sports folks. If you're at work and you're at your computer, and you have some guy yelling at you from across the room, "You suck!", you couldn't put together a PowerPoint presentation to save your life. Or "What did your mother do to you that you don't know how to revise these sales figures?" That behavior wouldn't last one day. Neither would the person yelling it.

I mean, what is the point of heckling somebody who's playing a sport? If you are a true fan, you are there to support the team, cheer them on, see some action, and enjoy the event. But hecklers seem to think they are the real fans because they see themselves as part of the action.

Excuse me?

If you see yourself as one of this special breed of superfan, let me see if I understand properly. You believe you're part of the action because you sit there with a hot dog in one hand and a beer in the other screaming, "You suck!" Or "Your wife is . . . whatever." Uh-huh . . . I see . . . Now, is there a spring training camp for that particular talent? Do they bring you along on the team plane for away games? No? Strange . . .

What do you gain from that trash talk? Nothing. And you might be buying yourself some trouble. Pros tune it out. OK, there was that time Ron Artest went into the stands, but that doesn't happen often. Are you willing to test that?

It amazes me that people are always surprised when they have driven someone to a breaking point. If you are a trash talker, have you thought this through? Not every player's gonna go, "Oh, OK. That's cool, you're just heckling me." Some guys aren't going to take it well. And some just might come up into the stands and get in your face. And then what are you going to do? Because you can't beat them. You have no place to run. And even if you did . . . are you going to outrun a pro athlete?

Good luck, superfan.

It never used to be like this. All right, maybe when I was a kid, you'd hear, "Get outta there, ya bum!" Maybe you'd hear that. But you wouldn't hear, "Hey, you frickin' idiot, your mother is a blah-blah-blah." People didn't do that. And they didn't do it because it wasn't right.

At the bottom line of it all, you're there to watch the game. And if you don't want to see the game, then why did you go? Other people might actually want to see it, and it's not OK that you go and mess up their evening with their child. An evening when they shelled out good money for the seats, the parking, the food, everything. It's not cheap.

Here's the thing. My answer to it . . . Want to be an ass? Stay home! Be an ass inside your house. Yell and scream at the TV all you want. Don't go screwing up somebody else's good time because, A, you've had too much to drink, or B, you don't know how to act in public.

Fan ugliness is everywhere. When the Yankees were playing the Phillies in the World Series, the New York papers had the nastiest pictures and headlines right on the cover. Real taunting, you know, just sort of stepping on their manhood. What is that?

Those players were visiting in New York with their families. Why should they have to look at pictures of themselves in skirts? Or the picture they Photoshopped of Pedro in the baby diaper.

It seems wrong to me. Just wrong.

And when a newspaper does that, it sort of validates it for the punks who go to the game to heckle Derek Jeter, thinking he's going to hear every word they say. Heckle Jeter? Let me hip you to this, dear heckler:

You are a flea on the ass of a mosquito on Derek Jeter's jersey. That's what you are.

Play Nice or Stay Home

Rude fans at sports stadiums don't stop at heckling. Hell, no. Why should they be satisfied merely yelling trash about a player's mother's STDs (yikes!), when they can step it up to an arrest for disorderly conduct?

These people are jackasses. Plain and simple But come on . . . we both know it's more than that. I'm going out on a limb here. I'm going to say that I believe these . . . offensive individuals . . . may have some special help. And I think it's alcohol.

What?? Get outta town . . .

These losers are somewhere on the scale between "Buzzed" and "Hammered Off Their Asses." And here's the thing . . . If you can't hold your alcohol, you should not be at the game. Drinking. That's it right there. You should not be at the game drinking if you cannot hold your liquor.

For the longest time until it was finally stopped, the old Giants Stadium in the Meadowlands had a weekly gathering of about five hundred drunks near the infamous Gate D, harassing women every Sunday football game. It was a total mob mentality. And people would wonder, how did five hundred people get away with that for so long?

I know why. It's exactly because there were five hundred of them. Call it vulgarity in numbers. Because if no one gets reported, or nobody gets in trouble, a guy figures, "Well, if I'm with them, I can't get in trouble either. They can't find me in five hundred other people." And when you include alcohol in that, man . . . Alcohol tends to make people believe that it's OK for them to do or say anything.

Duh.

But, oh, what stunts they pull . . . Like the fans who like to pack batteries in snowballs and throw them at the football players. That's just dangerous. What gives anybody the right to come in and throw a brick dressed as a snowball at somebody and think it's funny? What if they hit him? That's one player going to the hospital and one fan going to jail.

The hot new summer sport doesn't seem to be baseball. It's fans running out onto the field to be Tasered by cops. Why? . . . Really, why??

What makes people think they have the right to leave their house and go to some stadium and be obnoxious?

Stay home.

Who decided a stadium is a free pass? I think a lot of people believe it is. It's the "If It Happens in Vegas" mentality . . . only in the bleachers.

How about when you're sitting there and folks show up with all sorts of crap and start spreading it out on the seats like it was a sale? They spread out like they were in their living rooms or Man Caves at home. If you're one of these people, here's The Big Question: What gives you the right to go to a stadium and pretend you're at home? And if you have a Man Cave? You may already be a lost cause.

I bet you don't pull anything like that at home. I doubt that they would let you. And maybe that's why you're moving around to ball parks and stadiums so much. You think that you're *entitled* to do it because you paid $490 for a ticket? What about the other people who paid for tickets too? What are they entitled to? What if everybody does it?

It's nuts.

Now, there are some annoyances at sporting events that you can't really do anything about. For instance, some folks complain that they don't like it when people keep getting up and down during the game 'cause they make everybody stand up and move every two minutes. I say, let that one go. It's annoying, but you don't know if they have to go to the bathroom or get food or maybe just walk off a leg cramp from being crowded by that guy who spread his crap out all over the row. That's one we just relax and live with. Choose your battles.

If you want to get angry at someone, save it for the fans who think it's cute to harass or belittle the food and souvenir vendors . . . giving them demeaning nicknames, or tossing their money so they have to stoop for it. They think it's funny. But everything's a little more amusing when you're buzzed.

Most people don't know how to drink. I'm going to take a wild guess that these are not the people paying attention to the end of the TV ad where it says, "Enjoy responsibly."

They enjoy being jerks.

Meanwhile, these stadium vendors are working stiffs. They're not enjoying a Sunday afternoon in a reserved seat pounding back a cold brew. They're the ones serving it. Carrying fifty or sixty pounds on their backs, making change while some joker makes fun of them.

I'm a sports fan. I'm supposed to come to this game and enjoy myself and cheer my team. You, however, are not supposed to be throwing things and acting up right next to me. Or leaning over my kid and being rude. You're not supposed to do that.

I have an idea for a new tradition at the stadium. Throwing out the first drunk.

Stadium Behavior

Have you ever been involved in an altercation with another fan at a sporting event?

   If no, score 0

   If once, score 2

   If more than once, score 5

Have you ever been spoken to by stadium security about your drinking, swearing, or rowdiness?

   If no, score 0

   If yes, score 5

   If you don't remember, score 10

If stadium security cautioned you, did it bother you that they did?

   If yes, score 0

   If no, score 5

Have you ever thrown an object onto the field (or floor or ice)?

   If no, score 0

   If yes, score 5

Have you ever been asked to leave a sporting event because your behavior was disruptive to other fans?

   If no, score 0

   If yes, score 5

   If more than once, score 10

Did you care?

    If yes, score 0

    If no, score 5

If someone disrupted your time at the game, would it bother you?

    If yes, score 0

    If no, score 5

Total score: _____

Tally your score and write it in on the Master Score Sheet
at the back of this book, page 195.

Block That Parent

What is wrong with soccer moms and Little League dads? No, no, hang on. Not all of them. I'm talking about the ones you see verbally or physically abusing their kids' coaches and referees at games.

Hey, sideline moms and baseball dads . . . What is wrong in your life that you have to go and yell at people like that? And know what makes it worse? These coaches are often just volunteering to do this job. These aren't paid referees. These aren't paid coaches. These are folks who give of their time so kids get a chance to play a team sport. So why abuse them? If you have a real issue with a coach, report him to the league. You don't have to stand there screaming at him . . . looking like a freak.

Yeah, a freak. You see, from an onlooker's perspective, there isn't anybody who looks so fine doing that. Nobody looks good doing it.

What's changed here? It used to be when you got into Little League and youth soccer it was all about teaching kids something. Playing and values . . . Teamwork . . . How to be good sports . . . Having fun. I don't know what it's about now. I don't get it. I don't get why parents don't see what they're doing, acting out like they do.

And doesn't it ever once occur to them that this is not the behavior you want to teach a kid? They get all pissed off when their kid is rude, but their rudeness is OK? . . . Am I the only one not getting this?

Unlike bad stadium behavior, this usually doesn't involve alcohol. Usually. It's an ego thing, or about parents living their dreams through their kid . . . whatever. It's a little sad. Because then the poor kid's trying to figure out, "Well, is this OK behavior? . . . Must be.

My parents are doing it. So then it must be all right if I do it to my sister or I do it to kids at school." If you are one of these nightmare parents, ask yourself—are you showing your child how to become a bully?

Obviously, this behavior is widespread. Don't take my word for it. Go to a ball field and look at the signs warning parents how to behave. Think about that. They have to put up signs.

What is happening?

Some soccer leagues have instituted something called Silent Sidelines. They're trying to deal with parents who can't contain themselves by making a rule that parents can't cheer either. I see. That's the solution to stopping the heckling?

What the hell?! Something's out of whack here. They're shutting everybody up because of a handful of pissants? Enjoy your game, kids.

I think this is a better solution. If you're a player who is belligerent, the consequence should be that you can't be on the team. If your parents are belligerent, they can't bring you there to play. Most parents, when faced with the annoyance of their child—complaining because their ridiculous behavior has gotten their kid kicked off the team and unable to play anywhere else for a year—would probably learn to keep their big mouths shut.

If there were consequences for belligerence, would people behave differently? They might . . .

But there aren't consequences, and so we see this pestilence sort of rolling around the world. People just saying anything they feel like, or behaving any way they feel like. Yelling at the coach, "You're ignoring my son!!" But there are twelve other kids on the team. Don't they count?

I think they do. Too bad I'm not the one who needs to know that.

Sideline Civility

At your child's game, has anyone asked you to chill, that it's only a game?
   If no, score 0
   If yes, score 3

On the sidelines or bleachers, do other parents ever move away from you?
   If no, score 0
   If yes, score 5

Has your child-athlete ever asked you to stop yelling or not to fight with the other parents?
   If no, score 0
   If yes, score 5
   If more than once, score 10

Did it bother you that your child asked that?
   If yes, score 2
   If no, score 5

Have you ever called your child's coach a curse name, or threatened the coach?
   If no, score 0
   If yes, score 10

Would it piss you off if someone did that to you?
   If yes, score 2
   If no, score 5

Total score: _____

Tally your score and write it in on the Master Score Sheet
at the back of this book, page 195.

Down in Front!

How many times do you go to your kid's school pageant or a dance recital or graduation and there's this proud parent who has decided to be Steven Spielberg . . . Some mom or dad with a camera . . . shooting video, getting up, roaming around up to the stage, and so forth . . . Listen, I'm cool with that. I am. We're all proud of our kids and want to capture the moment. Groovy. Shoot away!

But . . . don't get in front of me. If I'm a parent in that audience, I want to see my kid too. And now, you're in my way, Mr. Spielberg. And I don't like it. So do what you've got to do, get your pictures, but don't obscure other people's sight. Don't make others suffer for your "art."

If you are one of these videographers, I have to ask something. What makes your . . . *Little Documentary That Could* . . . more important than everyone else's chance to enjoy a moment at their child's event?

And, in case you got too caught up in your cinematic moment to notice, you are incredibly embarrassing. Parents think it's cute but it is amazing to me that they don't remember how they felt when this was done to them. Even though it was with a Polaroid or a Kodak Brownie.

And for kids trying to perform on that stage, it sure doesn't help their concentration. It can't be good for them. In fact, it's probably freaking them out. So you go ahead making your digital masterpiece. Memorialize a performance where your child is traumatized because she sees you skulking around. Oh, and get her reaction when she also notices all the other people who are looking at you, going, "I wish this goofball would sit down."

But mostly, all your kid hears is, "Whose parent is that?"

Make sure you get all that on video.

Manners

You know, it's tough to see little courtesies, once so common in our lives, slide away like they have. Now, I call these courtesies little, but they aren't so little.

For instance, "please" and "thank you" are powerful words. You want something? Ask for it nicely. I don't care whether it's in the fanciest restaurant or at the counter of your favorite fast-food spot in the lunchtime rush, notice how adding a "please" at the end of your order can bring a smile? Or when a stranger takes a moment to stop and hold a door open for us, "Hey, thanks" matters. I know if I didn't say it, I wouldn't feel right. It's just an acknowledgment that you are paying attention.

It takes two seconds and it means the world.

So why aren't people bothering with manners anymore? I mean, we used to have them, right?

It starts young. For them, it's not so much that they're being rude. They don't know any better.

Kids learn by rote. Let's just say when children are around un-civil people—especially adults with no manners—well, do I need to tell you what hits the fan?

That's the sound we're hearing. And there's only two choices. Basic politeness and common courtesy, or rudeness and incivility.

Case in point: Let's take the health care debate. We saw people lose their minds! Really . . . People spitting on folks . . . Yelling ugly things—the N-word, the F-word . . . Sending death threats. You wonder . . . do these folks have kids? Do they care their kids might see them on TV or acting like asses? And are their kids going to grow up to reflect their parents' creepy behavior when they don't like what someone says?

When I was a kid, man, if you didn't say "please" or "thank you" or "excuse me" instead of "Huh?" some adult would come flying into that room and be all up in your face demanding to know if you had been brought up by savages!!!

And you had to be polite about stuff you hated. You were taught to at least be civil about that ugly, awful birthday present from some aunt you never heard of, but she was on the phone and you had to talk to her right then and say thank you, because your folks or the adults didn't want your bad manners to reflect on them.

Gadzooks.

I mean, think about it. It was "Yes, sir," "No, ma'am," and "Hello, Mr. and Mrs. So-and-so." You'd never call an adult by their first name because it was considered disrespectful.

So when we grew up, a lot of us decided, "The hell with that. My kids will be raised not having to do those things. We will be friends and they will call my adult friends by their first names and I will reason with them and not sweat the manners so much."

That was a mistake because we didn't realize, with manners, we must start young.

An Elevator Is
Like a Bathroom

I like people. Crowds . . . ? Uh . . . no thanks.

For instance, there's a special place in my heart for people who love to stand right in front of me, blocking that escalator while they check their cell phones. No there isn't. Same as there isn't for the hand-holders . . . those groups of people who walk—no, saunter—four or five abreast on a sidewalk like it's some . . . I don't know . . . sweep operation.

The elbows-out people are lots of fun too. It's not enough that they are loitering in a narrow aisle of the store . . . Why not super-size the obstruction by putting both hands on the hips and poking those wings out? And then they walk a circle, just to add to the sport. Score an extra ten points if they are wearing huge back-packs and earphones so they can't hear your polite request to get their butt out of the way . . . By saying, "Excuse me, please," of course. Of course!

Moving around well on foot is a lost art. When I was a kid and you walked down the sidewalk with a guy, he was always supposed to be on the street side. They say it was a throwback to the days when the streets were not well paved and a gentleman didn't want the woman to get splashed by water from a passing car. I thought it was kind of dopey but, hey . . . at least everybody knew where to be.

On subways or commuter trains, there's an unwritten law of flow for that too. Although . . . as you have probably noticed . . . a lot of people don't seem to know it. Maybe because it's an unwrit-ten law. So as a public service, let me write it here:

When you're getting onto a subway, wait for the people to get off.

Simple as that. Astoundingly, crowds still try to get out *and* in at the same time. Know what that is called? That is called a line of scrimmage. It makes no sense and drives people crazy. Why don't people wait for everyone to get off first? It's because they're afraid they're not going to get on. Listen. If they would just step to the side so that people don't have to push them out of the way to get off of the thing, chances are they would actually get on *faster* because it would be a clear path. It's not only polite, it's common sense. But who says we have a surplus of those two things? Not I.

I guess the same thing applies to people getting on and off of elevators. Another peeve of mine. Yours too? Need I ask?

Ninety percent of people waiting for an elevator stand in front of the friggin' door. How come? Because they're not thinking that maybe . . . just maybe . . . other people are going to be on that elevator, and they're probably going to want to get off. Generally, the dance step is to stand to the side so everybody can get off without having to collide with a wall of humanity. Just like subways, elevators are give-and-take spaces. And work best in that order, meaning . . . give before you take.

Like life itself.

And if you're already on the elevator, standing in front of the panel, sing out. Ask people what floor they want. Most folks are cool about this. In my experience, most people who are in front of the panel will ask . . . If not, just speak up and say, "Would you press three for me, please?"

"Please?" Wow. They won't know what to do.

Elevators are awkward spaces. You get in there and what are you supposed to do? You're supposed to just sort of stand there until you get where you're going. But folks are always uncomfortable. People get onto an elevator and they're not smiling, so that makes people even more uncomfortable. They think, "OK, now I've got to stand here with this . . . stranger."

The elevator is like the bathroom. Once you're in there, you have a few moments to think about what you need to do. And other people can make it feel uncomfortable. That's why people get so annoyed when people are speaking loudly on the elevator. It's also irritating when someone gets on wearing earbuds cranking music at max volume. It's probably why they don't pump in Muzak anymore. Who needs the Percy Faith Orchestra playing "Muskrat Love" when you can enjoy the tinny crap bleeding out of the Human Resources guy's skull?

It's also like the bathroom because people avoid eye contact. Those doors close and folks suddenly get elevator eyes. That's because, I find, most people don't know how to interact in that little box. So when you smile and say, "Hey." They go, "Oh . . . somebody's talking . . . What? Oh, hey." There is nothing wrong with a little "How you doin', hey." And, you know, it does make the day a tiny bit brighter when you get on an elevator and you're greeted.

You don't have to have a deep, personal relationship with this person. But it's just acknowledgment. Just to acknowledge I'm in this tiny little space with you. And that we're all uncomfortable. But it'll be all right.

And now that that's done, everybody stare up at the numbers . . .

Encourage Your Kids
to Play by Themselves

Somebody sent me this wonderful thing for my birthday . . . an observation about the differences between generations. One of them said if you were born between 1930 and 1969, you grew up going outside and staying out from eight o'clock in the morning in the summertime until five o'clock. And no one was freaked out that you weren't home. Nobody. That's true. We did all kinds of things because our parents demanded that we go outside and socialize.

"Get out and play!"

You had to do it. And you know what happened? You learned how to make friends. You learned how to navigate . . . well . . . Life.

For some reason, children now are not taught how to be independent. As a kid, because I had to go out and play, I knew the outside world. This generation knows a computer screen. They don't seem to know they can go outside.

There's a generation of parents now who hardly get to see who their kids are friends with. Because they don't come to your home. They're all on the computer. You have to take your kid's word for it that they're even real people.

We had imaginary friends. Theirs are virtual.

So there are certain aspects of all of this that are really hard for me and a lot of people to understand. And somehow, folks younger than me—parents that are younger than me—don't seem to remember the days of having to go outside and play. The days when you got out there and met people . . . and dealt with the world.

You know, back when you went to the library—the what??

Yeah. And not the library that was a folder on your computer's desktop. The library that was a place. The library where you had to interact with—the librarian! You had to learn how to ask questions. You had to wait. Your. Turn. You had to learn how to navigate where you were. You learned how to do it by going . . . By getting out there and having to do the work—in person. It's just a very different time now.

Many parents now don't understand what their kids are studying in school. So there isn't a way to engage because the adults don't follow what the kids are doing. You can't be as involved as you would like if you don't understand it yourself. So that connection is fading. "Mom, can you help me with my homework?" is a rarity now.

They don't really need you as much anyway, because they can go on the frickin' computer and figure it all out. Technology seems to have helped them be able to learn everything independently . . . except how to *be* independent people like we had to be. Computers have made it easier for them in one way, but you know what? They have also made it tougher because doing everything online has robbed them of experiences.

It's why it's important for parents to say things like "please" and "thank you." And "may I?" And to talk about what's in the news and what's happening in the world. And to travel and spend time out there. Yes—Out There!

It's why it's important that kids learn about having friends, so that if they do go to somebody's house, they know how to speak to the parents. How to interact with actual people.

Maybe even how to tell time when it's not digital.

Peer Itself

Children and parents are not peers. As I mentioned earlier, when I was a kid, we had to call everybody Mr. and Mrs. So-and-so. It's the acknowledgment of another person and their place in the hierarchy. Southern people do it all the time. Miss So-and-so. And people always enjoy a laugh about it. That's because it's one part respectful, one part wink. Mostly, though, it's respectful.

But, listen up. Your son's or daughter's friends . . . those kids are not your equals! Unfortunately, I think a lot of agitation comes because adults don't know how to get respect.

When a kid comes over and the adult says, "Call me Steve," you're setting up a relationship that may or may not work. It's hard to know. Every relationship is different, and blahdy-blahdy-blah. Got it . . . But. I do think going back to some of the basics might help. Now, do I want to be addressed as Miss Goldberg by folks? No, not everybody. But, see, I have the kind of name that is meant for people to call it, big and small, just what it is. Whoopi. You know?

But your son's or daughter's friends, they should call you "Mr." or "Mrs." Just out of respect. Don't assume that you can be, or should be, their best friend.

It's like they say about music. If you learn the rules, you know when you're breaking them. And I think you need to start young knowing the rules of how we interact. Then, maybe decide when . . . and when *not* . . . to break them. But you've got to have the rules, I think. And kids need to know they mean something. And that comes from the adults.

Remember when most of us were kids? You did not have control over the telephone. So if you were in deep doo-doo, your parents said, "You know what? Your friends cannot call." And that was that. Remember that? There was no explaining, and adults did not care if you were mad. And you could not talk back because there were Big Repercussions.

One of the other things that people never used to do when I was a kid, was adults never used to talk about other adults in front of kids. Don't do it! It's wrong to talk or gossip about an adult in front of a child. Then, next thing you know, it gets around to other kids. With information you may or may not have correct.

It's like having a kid hear an adult say, about someone, "Well, what's wrong with her? Why doesn't she want more kids? Doesn't she like kids?" Maybe it doesn't occur to people maybe she can't afford to have more kids. There could be a million reasons. But why call her out in public? Especially in front of a child!

I've found when you're dealing with little kids, they really do operate mostly based on what they see. They are responsible if you are responsible. They understand things if—*if*—you can keep it child-friendly and short.

Now, I made a mistake in my earlier years thinking that because I was explaining stuff to my daughter that, at seven and eight, she was putting it in her brain computer. Well, that's all well and good but at seven and eight they don't really know what your experience at twenty-eight or thirty or forty has been. So just because you tell them something, and they give you the look that says, "Yes, I get it" . . . doesn't mean that they get it.

When she was young I said to my daughter, "Look, I'm going to go and I'm going to be on Broadway." And she's like, "OK." Then, when I was gone, she'd say, "Where are you? Why aren't you here?" And I'd say, "I explained it to you." "OK, you explained it, but it doesn't mean anything to me. I'm eight years old." And that was a very clear message to me. I had to admit that I was just trying to do what I wanted and I tried to get her to go along so I could do what I wanted to do and not feel guilty. Really, what I wanted was permission. Now I know you can't do that.

Most parents, if they say, this is what I'm doing, a kid will say, "OK," and not really understand what it entails. All the sacrifices that they are going to have to make. Or the demands on your time. It's important. And parents . . . you've got to know that kids are not going to understand what you're going through. They're just not. They don't have your experience. And if they don't understand what you're going through, they have no clue as to how it's going to affect them. So you sort of have to be a little more realistic than I was.

And this was a huge lesson for me. I still had to be the parent. You have to have the relationship that allows you to be the adult. Where you actually have to take responsibility. You know, we can talk about responsibility with kids as much as we want to, but the truth of the matter is you're the adult. You are responsible. When they're seven and eight you can't ask them to be responsible. You can ask them to be responsible for homework. But you can't ask them to be responsible for how you're doing. Or how you're feeling. It just isn't their responsibility to take care of you. It's your responsibility to take care of them.

And you have to be measured, I think, in the things that you say to them. Because they don't need to have all of the information all of the time. They need a lot of the information . . . and often. And there's a difference. And they are not mini-adults. They're not little forty-year-olds. They're seven, eight, and nine. And all those things that you were when you were seven, eight, and nine. That's what they get to be too.

So by not sharing that global stuff, you let them still be kids.

Now. There are some things, some moments in life, as we discovered on September 11, 2001, where you've got to say, "I don't know." Because suddenly, everybody was reduced to childhood on September 11. Nobody could understand it. It was foreign to us. And so, you know, if it was foreign to us and you're in your forties, it's way foreign to little ones if they're seven and eight.

If things like that are happening in the world, they don't need to see it on TV all the time. They don't need to relive it over and over and over again.

Those towers came down more than once. Hundreds of times, thousands of times, on the television. I just sort of feel like there are some things that you're going to have to admit that you don't know how to respond to. And that it's something you'll just have to discover together.

Role Models Will Disappoint You

When a famous person gets his ass handed to him in a public scandal, people just can't get enough of the dirt. But then in the same breath, they shake their heads and say, "Pity too. He was such a role model."

Drives me crazy.

This isn't *Dirty Laundry* by Don Henley. This is real people's lives.

And tell me something . . . Why do we have to discuss it 24/7? The truth of the matter is, there is no privacy anywhere. For anyone. Not when there is an entire industry that makes its fortune off of the misfortune of others.

And why is that considered OK? Am I the only one who is bothered that, in our society, instant damnation is the standard? "Off with his head!" . . . That's become the starting point. Not, "Man, that's really too bad." Or, "I wonder if it's true?" We start out with the premise that it is true. You used to be innocent until proven guilty. Until *proven* guilty.

What the hell is this idea of role models, anyway? I have a news flash. Role models are not who you want to be seeking out as blueprints for your life. If you are looking for a direction to go, you don't want to be looking outside. Who is your role model?

You are.

Celebrity role models will just disappoint you. Know why? Because, in truth, they are role mortals. Humans.

And this is a big, dangerous thing. If you can't assess right and wrong . . . what's right for you . . . because you're going to pattern yourself after someone else, here's a question: Does that mean that they're responsible if it doesn't work out for you? See, just because I have lived my life a certain way is no guarantee that you're going to have the same luck. So are you going to be pissed at me because it didn't work out for you? You may find yourself rudely disappointed to discover there's a lot I can get away with that you can't. It's a very, very tricky thing.

But the bottom line is this. A role model is really not—cannot be—someone who is not you. Because the only control you really have is of yourself.

If you are a parent, you might be wondering, OK then, how can my child learn to be his or her own role model? There is no simple answer. And know what? That is the whole point. Oh, man, if only it were as easy as patterning yourself after an icon. But it isn't. So talk with your young ones. Let them know that it's all inside, not outside. That's where the values are.

Maybe it's more mirror . . . less TV.

Tiger Woods. He never said he was a role model. He never said he was anything but a great golfer. And that's all he's obligated to be. Now, you like his life? You want to pattern yourself after him? OK, but it may not work out. (You may not have heard, but he's had a few difficulties.)

What about Adam Lambert? He did what he was supposed to do on *American Idol*. Now . . . he's openly gay and has always been sort of goth. Chances are he's going to do things differently than someone else. So someone can't boo-hoo if they watched a TV show where he was doing something shocking on stage and felt let down by their role model.

These people are only entertainers entertaining you.

Or athletes.

Or people you see on television or in films or on the news.

And remember . . .

We don't know them. And we cannot be pissed off when they are not who we think they're supposed to be. Wouldn't you be mad as hell if somebody looked over at you and said, "I've made you my role model and, therefore, you have to behave in the way I think you're supposed to behave"? No one wants to hear that.

There's big money in role models. Somebody's known as a good golfer, and suddenly he's the Wristwatch Person.

Except, you know what? He is the Wristwatch Person because he plays golf. But the marketing people think, "Well, if folks like the way he plays golf, they'll want to wear what he wears. They'll want to drive what he drives. They'll want to invest the way that he invests."

This has nothing to do with his character. They are selling an image to people who want to identify with a role model. That's their deal. All the golfer does is swing the club and wear the freakin' watch. That is the relationship.

That is the role.

Tiger Woods, as far as I can see, is just a great golfer.

I guess the question you want to be asking yourself is . . . what are you?

Role Models Who Have Disappointed Us

Not all of them are bad people. Some just hit bumps because they are mere mortals. Many of them have bounced back. But at one time or other, these so-called role models have made us go, "Say it ain't so . . ."

- Tiger Woods

- O. J. Simpson

- Bernard Kerik

- Pete Rose

- Mark McGwire

- Sammy Sosa

- Lindsay Lohan

- Amy Winehouse

- John Mayer

- Whitney Houston

- Michael Phelps

- Kanye West

- Britney Spears

- Heidi Montag

- Michael Vick

- John Edwards

- Paris Hilton

- Miley Cyrus

- Chris Brown

- Eliot Spitzer

- Rush Limbaugh

- Benedict Arnold

- Vince "ShamWow" Shlomi (if you're curious, look it up)

This list means nothing . . .
    . . . As long as you are not on it.

How Do I Look?
And Tell the Truth

If you're a woman, and you don't want the truthful answer to a question . . . don't ask it! Just don't.

"Does this dress make me look fat?" might be one to avoid.

Now—you could always say, "I need you to lie to me right now." Personally, if I were in a relationship with someone and asked that, guess what? . . . I would love that man so much more if he said, "Yeah, baby, it does make you look fat. And it doesn't look that good on you."

He's my man, why would he lie?

Because as hot as you think you look, if your old man doesn't think you look hot, and he's walking behind you going, "Oh, my God, her ass is hanging out," *you are not looking hot.*

Flattery isn't good behavior. Flattery is sometimes dishonest behavior. Come again? Didn't anybody ever read *The Emperor's New Clothes?*

Women, do not ask the question unless you want to hear the truth. Because the only time I ask, "Do I look weird in this?" is when I want somebody to tell me, A, no you don't. Or, B, you do. And I only ask people whose opinions I actually care about.

And to me, those things are important. When it's more important that you're lied to in a relationship . . . check yourself. Something's wrong.

Now, what I've heard on *The View* is that—apparently—women don't want the truth, so men don't tell the truth to women about how they look. They just lie.

I don't understand it.

Why wouldn't you want the person that you spend the most amount of time with . . . or the person that you sleep with . . . to tell you the truth—that you don't look good and to change your clothes? Why would you want that person to let you out of the house looking like hell?

Why wouldn't you want to know that man thinks enough of you to say, "Listen, that does not flatter you. You don't look good in that. Especially when you turn that way. You look like the side of a building. That's not the right thing for you to wear if you want to look good. And I don't care if you bought it and you thought you looked good . . . You don't! I'm telling you. You've got the sides fat there, you've got the belly fat there, I can see your stuff, your stuff is hanging . . ."

OK, maybe that's too much truth. But you catch the drift . . . Right?

If you ask the opinion of someone you care about, you should be prepared to hear the truth and not be angry. And if you are angry, is it at him for being honest, or are you mad because you knew when you had to squeeze into that (because you've put on a few pounds), that it might not work out the way you wanted?

But see, once you put that conversation in another person's hands, it's no longer what *you* want. It's not about you anymore. It's about you saying, "You fulfill my fantasy, but will you please fulfill it the way I wish you would fulfill it?"

And if you want a relationship based on "wishful truthing," where does it end? Clothes? . . . That is just the beginning.

If you ask, "Am I the best you ever had?" be prepared, because the honest answer could be, "Well, no . . . But you're the best for me right now. And here's what you can do better for me, and here's what I think I can do better for you. You want to tell me what I can do better for you? I will try to do that."

Now *that's* a conversation.

Working through this is hard. A relationship is the day-to-day work. The hour-to-hour, the minute-to-minute stuff. And usually . . .

just asking one question about something small can suddenly lead you onto some very rough road. If you want the truth, buckle up.

Which is probably why everyone just told the emperor his threads were cool.

The Three Questions

All right, I'm going to try to help you out with something here. You do want some practical skills after reading this book, right? I mean, it can't all be beauty and entertainment.

What I've got to share with you is one way to keep yourself from slipping into one of the nastiest of bad habits.

Gossip.

Yeah, sure, I know all that is just human nature. Is it the best of human nature?

No. And it affects so many.

We are all vulnerable to snooping and running our mouths off about things that aren't any of our business. So to fight off the urge, stop and ask yourself three simple questions:

1. Does it put any food on your table?

2. Does it enhance your life in any way?

3. Does it affect your personal being?

If you answer "No" to any of these . . .

Butt out.

And it ain't easy . . . believe me, I know. Every day I know. I'm human too. I feel the pull to check out the latest gossip. Maybe just one bitty peek. You know what it's like. It's a constant struggle not to succumb to the Dark Side.

Most days I win, but many days I don't.

But I keep trying.

You Realize I Can See You

I smoke. And this is one of those things that gets me sort of nuts. If you're standing outside, and you're smoking because you've been forbidden to smoke anywhere—except in this microscopic patch of area—people walk by you . . . and wave their hands in the air.

The commentary is unnecessary.

Why? Because people are already standing outside feeling like criminals to start with. Inside, it's made very clear:

"If you smoke in this room YOU WILL GO TO JAIL!"

It's pretty deep. But people walk by and they cough. And I always want to say, "What point is there to you coughing? What is this supposed to do except piss me off?"

So why would they do it?

We hear all about the smokers who don't have manners and how they get smoke in other people's faces. But there's no conversation at all about smokers who have complied—and yet they are still getting crap!!

If you are one of these self-deputized, self-righteous smoking vigilantes, I want to talk to you. And I want to ask, what is the effect on your life if I am standing outside in twenty-one degrees—alone—smoking?

Does my cigarette bother you, or is it the idea of my cigarette?

And what is going on here? Why have we lost the ability to hold our opinions to ourselves when someone is doing something that is legal? As much criticism as there is about smoking, *it's still legal*. If you are of age, you can go in and buy cigarettes. And do you know why? Because no state is going to get rid of smoking because . . . they want the revenue. So I question the health czars who say, "Oh, smoking's bad for you," and yet your state—your legislature—isn't getting rid of the cigarettes because they want the tax money.

So really now . . . Does anyone really care what I'm doing?

Which is it? Because you can't have it both ways. You can't be pro my health and then put cigarette ads out everywhere. And keep selling them.

And you know what else? You don't have to exacerbate a situation because you're feelin' prissy.

Think about this. We agree that people have positive and negative opinions about drinking, right? Right. But it is still legal if you are of age . . . just like cigarettes. Follow along with me. What would it be like if you were quietly enjoying a cocktail, and someone came into the bar and went, "You know, you're gonna hit something because you've had that drink. You're a drunk."

Or if they walked by and did a hiccup instead of the cough.

People smoke, and they're going to continue to smoke. It's like people drink, and they're going to continue to drink. Smokers already know the rap, that's why they're outside like criminals. Someone doing the right thing . . . complying with the rules and standing in two-degree weather . . . doesn't need a comment from you.

Why do you even need to? What is it doing for you? Does it make you feel better? What's wrong in your life? That's what you should be thinking about.

If I'm over in the corner smoking my cigarette, leave me alone. Leave me alone. I'm away from you because you say cigarettes bother you, but you make it a point to be close enough to comment so I hear you, so I guess you can't be that concerned, because you're over here.

And what are you trying to do anyway, start a fight? There are some people who get very upset about this. They say, "This is the one thing in my day . . . I've been in that cubicle . . . waiting for this moment. My cigarette break. And now you're ruining it. And why are you surprised if I get in your face?"

See, these are things that get me all worked up too, because I'm not bothering anyone. And what I do in my personal life has no effect on others.

If you say, "Oh, I have asthma," or "I'm allergic," or "I can't breathe if you're smoking," most people will say, "OK, I'll go outside or I won't smoke by you." But this idea that all smokers—all people who smoke—are easy targets just makes me nuts.

Now. If somebody's clipping their toenails on the train, you get to comment on that. You get to actually go, "Could you not do that?" Because it's unsanitary. I don't know where your feet have been. I don't know what those claws are carrying. I don't know what you've been doing.

But if I'm outside, all by myself, enjoying my cigarette in peace . . . I'll make you a deal. I promise not to blow my smoke your way if you promise not to pretend I just did.

Hey . . . maybe we can make this work after all.

If You Don't Like It,
Don't Do It

Everybody's trying to tell us how to live our lives these days. It's annoying to me . . . In a big way. Here we are in a nation founded on personal liberty, but everywhere we turn there's either a finger wagging at us or a law being proposed to stop us from the pursuit of happiness.

And you know, it's more than annoying. It's kind of alarming, don't you think?

I say, if you don't like someone's behavior because he's cheating on his wife—then don't you do it. Don't worry about him. If you don't like it, don't you do it.

If you're concerned about gay people who want to get married . . . number one, don't marry a gay person! What does it do to you if two lesbians get married? What does it do to your faith? Nothing.

If you think abortion is bad—don't have one. But if I don't think it's bad? Don't you decide for me what I need. It's not your place.

And this is really the crux of this book. It's the crux of everything:

If you don't like it, don't do it.

You don't like to drink? You think alcohol is bad . . . then don't drink. But I like my alcohol. I like to have a glass of champagne. I don't want you all up in my business because I'm having a glass of the bubbly.

Out on the road, it's a whole different story.

If I'm getting in my car, and I've had a *bottle* of champagne . . . yeah, it would be a good idea for you to stop me. Because I could be affecting your life. *Then* it has something to do with you.

If you don't like violent TV—don't watch it.

If you don't like seeing sex on TV—don't watch it.

Same with the movies. You don't like all the violence—don't go see those movies.

Some people like a good, violent movie. Like *The Three Stooges*. It's violent. People getting hit all the time. You don't like it? Don't watch it. But don't take it away, because I do like it. And I haven't killed anybody or hurt anybody. If you have four examples of how it *may* affect some people, OK. We'll keep an eye out for those people who may have those symptoms. But I don't have those symptoms. So your decision to change what I do is really annoying

If you don't like red meat, don't eat it. If you're a vegan, eat your vegetables and be happy. But if I'm a steak 'n' potatoes girl . . . guess what? I don't want to hear from you. And I don't want you showing me pictures about how chickens and veal are butchered. I don't want to see it! And I don't see why you think it's OK to show it to me simply because you don't want me to do what I am enjoying.

If you don't like it—don't eat it.

I could see it if I had peanuts and you had a peanut allergy. Some people get anywhere near peanuts and it's . . . PHOOMPH . . . like, their skin falls off. That is understandable. But you're not saying to me, "You can't have peanuts." You're saying, "You can't have peanuts and make out with me." That's OK.

You don't want me to wear a fur coat? You don't like fur—don't wear it!

Why should somebody not affected by something decide what someone else can or can't do? People used to say to me, "Well, why did you buy that?" Well, why do you want to know? What do you care what I'm spending my money on? I'm not married to you. I am not your child. You are not my accountant. You have no business asking me that question.

"Wow, you paid that much for that?" Yeah . . . And?

You're mad. You're mad because I bought something with my money that I earned 'cause you think it's too much money to spend. But that's not my problem. That's your problem.

So it comes down to my money that I earned. My decisions. What I choose to do.

As long as it doesn't come into your house and mess with you—leave me alone. I'll go back to where I started . . . Doesn't it seem that what I'm talking about is the protection of our personal freedoms?

But here's the problem. One-on-one meddling in our private lives is irritating enough. This whole ugly "interference mentality" went to Washington and joined the debate over health care. You heard congressmen and senators deciding not to vote for it because it might cover something they don't like . . . Or want . . . Or find creepy.

Repeat after me: If you don't like it, don't do it.

You know, I listen to all these people who are still arguing that we never should have passed health care. Well, here's my take on that: In the next year, every senator and congressman who's against it should lose their benefits. They should all have to go out and get insurance like everybody else. And then they'd get it. Then they would understand it. It's like politicians who've never been to war sending kids to war. Sure, it's easy for them. If they've never been there, they might take a little more time before they made their decision. So if you have to fight tooth and nail to get your health benefits, I think you'd be a little more receptive to the pro side of the debate. You might understand why some systems might not work.

We heard the no's from people who have excellent health care. People who are covered every which way. They get a hangnail? They can go to the doctor. But so many other people don't have insurance and can't afford it. They can't get it because the decision is in the hands of people who have 100 percent insurance. So these guys and gals are still sitting around saying, "Aw, I don't think this is a good idea for the country . . ." I say turn the tables on them. Would that be fair? Would that be better if we said, "OK, you don't get to have *your* insurance. You have to have what we have. You have to take exactly the same routes that we have to take."

When President Obama addressed Congress, he said everybody should have what we have. What he should have said is, "We should have what they have." That's really what needs to happen. And that will spark a debate like you can't believe, because the minute people who have had the best can't have the best . . . there's a fight.

The point is health care reform was finally made law. But some people just won't let go of it. Too many things in it they don't like. Or want. Or find creepy. Well, they need to get past all that. Drop the shoe, Sparky!

Maybe they'll read this book. Or maybe you can tell them something for me:

If you don't like it, don't do it.

Should We Be Worried About This?

OK, we've all had this happen. We're ready to sit down and have dinner. The phone rings. It's your long-lost high school friend. "Guess who this is? . . . Really, guess! I ran into Jane at the supermarket and she gave me your number. I hope it's OK." Maybe it is OK. Maybe it's not. The fact is, it's a little late to ask that question.

Whoever gave your number out to that old high school classmate probably thought they were doing something kind for you. Or they were in the produce section and felt kind of put on the spot . . . Or maybe woozy from garlic fumes. The smarter thing to do—always—is to say, "You know what? Let me see if I can get hold of them." And call them and say, "I just ran into so-and-so, and they want your number. Do you want me to give it to them?" It only takes as long as it takes for you to write down the information.

Now, most people don't know what your relationship to that person is. Whether you're ready to talk to them, or whether you want to talk to them or be anywhere near them. And when you give out someone's personal information . . . whether it's an email address, a home address, or a phone number, you are potentially endangering them. Because you don't know what you're dealing with.

And even if you think, "Oh, I know this person wouldn't hurt her," the fact is, you don't know what the relationship to the person whose information you're giving out has been. So take a minute and just call or send an email making sure it's all right to share that info.

I'm a big believer in respecting personal boundaries. I try to respect other people's and I want them to respect mine . . . You do too, I bet. If not, please take a step back. Go back to the beginning of this book and start over.

I'm not just talking about people getting physically close or walking in your yard without your permission. That's another conversation. This is about personal information boundaries . . . and people need to respect those too. Including your friends and co-workers.

Think about what happens with your emails. You write them, you send them. Done, right? Nope. Because then what happens? People forward. So you send an email to somebody personal in your life. You've not only sent the text that you wrote to them, but if that gets forwarded, not only does your message get forwarded, so can your email address.

It's like this: I send an email to you. You say, I think Sherri would think this is funny. So you forward it to Sherri. Sherri then gets what I wrote—plus my email address. That's fine with me because Sherri's cool, but what if it's not Sherri? What if it's somebody I don't want to have all that? I didn't get a choice.

They have this thing called Blastmail, which is tech slang for a mass email from a mailing list. Now, say your friend sends out a Blastmail to you and thirty other people. Unless your friend knows how to mask them, every single one of those email addresses show up there too. So thirty other people, some of whom may be strangers, just got your email address. And you just got theirs. I just learned this . . . the hard way.

The privacy thing is only part of it. You know those little buttons for "Reply" and "Forward"? There's also one for "Reply All." Somebody clicks that, all thirty of you get their reply. Handy, I suppose, if you're working on a project with a large group. Or if you're a Baldwin or a Jonas and you want to make sure everybody in the family gets the word. But some folks get irritated when it's thirty responses to the joke about "You know you're over fifty when . . ." And then for the next three days you're getting emails coming to you from amateur comedians who pressed "Reply All."

I'm guilty of this. People send me wonderful, dopey emails that I love, so if I know other people that I think will like it, I send it to them.

But if you send out something that contains confidential information . . . it's all on you. So it's worth it to take a moment to read what you are sending. Then just make a new email without any of the sensitive content in it. That's an easy cut and paste job, and then you're covered.

I guess if people take the time and look at what they're doing before they send their emails out, a lot of hurt feelings can be avoided. The ladies on *The View* were talking about the fact that they have sent out emails to people by mistake. It's because they weren't paying attention. But it's too important not to. You've got to know what button you're clicking. You think you're forwarding but you're actually . . . replying?!? Uh-oh!

The Web is a great tool for communication. Unfortunately, it's just as great for miscommunication. Or a little too much communication.

This brings me to Tiger Woods. If nothing else came out of all that, it's learning that there are no borders in the digital world. If you put anything out there, you lose control of it. Someone can take it. And use it.

All those women say they have all of these texts between them. Now, with emails, I understand how you can save those. But a text message, I don't know how you physically save text messages for nine, ten, twelve months. Unless you're transcribing them. Or doing a cut and paste to email or Word. I'd like to know how they did that. How does that work? I need to know how to keep my texts for an entire year. Maybe I can do something with all those racy text messages Baby Elmo is always sending me.

Kidding!

But think about it. It just seems very odd of them to do that . . . to save all those supposed texts from him . . . For a year! What were they planning? I'm just curious. Just how does that work and should we all be worried about this? Because this is something that can potentially affect every person who uses texts.

You know, when you write a letter, people can keep them. So, I guess, any communication can be held. That is to say you could turn it into a booklet of the letters that were written to you. You could even turn them into dialogue for a musical. But now we have texts and we all have to start wondering, "Wow. Wow . . . How's that going to affect me?"

It's kind of spooky when you think about it. We suddenly get this new idea that you can't communicate without fear now. Anything you text—to anybody—is floating around like a big shoe that's waiting to drop.

Well, I guess people are starting to get hip to the problem, because they have come up with this new program, some app for cell phones that lets you make your text messages disappear from the other person's cell phone after they are read. It's kind of like the self-destruct thing at the beginning of *Mission: Impossible* . . . but without all the smoke. The maker's slogan is "Cover your tracks." Well, like they say, necessity is a mother.

They're calling this app *tigertext*.

Nuff said.

Bloggers Are Cowards

Not long ago, a blog published a story that the poet Maya Angelou couldn't appear at an awards event in Los Angeles because she had been rushed to the hospital. Instantly, the Web started buzzing. This was big. Twitter kicked in and, you know, next thing . . . word was out that Maya Angelou was dead. Her family and friends heard about it and started calling the house and panicking. She wasn't dead. She wasn't even in LA . . . which is almost as bad. She was in St. Louis, kicking back at her house.

This particular blog apologized for lighting the fuse on that story, but it's not the first blog to get it wrong in a big way. Another one famously posted a death speculation about Fidel Castro back in 2007. A bit premature.

The thing about these two bloggers, is that at least we know who they are. Shame on y'all!! But with most, you don't. They're anonymous. Anonymous assassins. They publish rumors and innuendo and sensational guesses. If it's about you, you're getting slammed left and right and you don't even know who it is.

And forget famous people. This is happening to you and your neighbors too. Even kids in school. Someone writes something on their friend's Facebook page about someone else. And *nobody* has to check it. But people see it and say, "Oh, this is a fact."

Bloggers are people who write stuff and no one has to check it. There's no one saying, "Is this accurate?" And true or not, once you say it in our wired-up society now, it travels around the world . . . four thousand times before noon.

Hey, you anonymous, unaccountable blogger. You're a coward. And my name is Whoopi Goldberg, if you're looking for me. I'm not scared to tell you that you're a coward because you hide. You don't want the effects of what you've said to come back and kick you in the ass. So there are no consequences. And because there are no consequences, you think you're absolutely free to say and do whatever you want. But what if there were consequences to this? . . . What if you had to register your real name? You'd have to take the heat that you stirred up.

And that means that you'd have to own the consequences of your actions. Or your words. Let the lawsuits begin!

When consequences disappear, civility goes out the door and anarchy takes over. If there is no consequence for bloggers doing damage, then they're just going to keep doing whatever they want to do . . . saying whatever they want to say. And who's to stop them?

What's that? Do I hear you saying wait a second? "Um—er, Whoopi? Isn't this a contradiction? Aren't you one moment talking about personal liberties like freedom of speech, and now here you are calling out bloggers for exercising theirs?"

You're right, I do prize freedom of speech. But last time I checked, freedom of speech doesn't mean you get to say any old thing you like. "Fire" in a theater and "bomb" in an airport are just two that come to mind. There are also libel and slander laws we all pretty much agree help protect folks from written and spoken abuses. And that's where I come down against the anonymous bloggers who do harm to people by spreading lies—without accountability—and think it's all cool just because it's on the Web.

Don't get me wrong, I like the Internet. But I don't love it. I like that I can find facts and information, but I don't like that anyone can say anything they want about people anonymously. But I do love it that some judge ruled that the anonymous blogger running *Skanks in NYC* had to reveal her identity to the ex-model who sued to find out who was talking shit about her. I think that's what it should be. I think you should have to be real. I don't think you should be able to post anonymously.

You want to talk shit? Face up.

It comes back to accountability. You should not be able to write just anything and have it circulate like that and not be held accountable for what you've written. I don't think it's good for adults . . . And I certainly don't think it's good for kids.

Remember, you don't have to be famous to have this happen to you. The best example of that, of course, was the security guard that they wrongly accused in the Atlanta bombings at the 1996 Olympics, Richard Jewell. That poor man's plight illustrated how you don't have to have your facts straight. And you can say it loudly and largely on paper, on television, everywhere.

And ruin a guy.

Don't Think You Know Someone Because You See Them on Television

Hey, so you're still with me! . . . Still reading, great. Thank you again. Can't say that too often . . . especially when you're banging on about civil behavior and manners and all. I wonder . . . Am I shocking a few people who got a copy of this book hoping to get all pissed off at me . . . only to find we've got more in common than they thought? If that's you, glad to bring you a little surprise . . . and, in the process, if I've made a new friend, that's great . . . If not, piss off.

I'm kidding. Sort of.

But you know, some people do want to be offended. Count on it . . . And that's because they have made up their minds about who I am. Do people do that with you? I mean, not really know you outside work or church once a week, and then . . . later . . . admit how different they find you? That's usually after a couple of margaritas and a laughing jag.

I never forget that . . . Oftentimes people like to think they know all about me because of what they've seen on TV. But, come on. You can't think you know me—or anyone—because of what comes at you from a flat screen.

This is inclusive of the people on *Survivor*, and *The Amazing Race*, and sitcoms, and *The Housewives of Boogah-Boogahville*, and whatever movies you've liked. Because unless you actually can have conversations with somebody, spend time with them . . . you don't know how their image has been put together. So sometimes you think you're walking up to somebody who thinks the way that you think.

Don't assume.

It's like me, for example. People paint me to be whatever makes *them* comfortable, so often they are shocked when they find out that . . . yeah, I am pro-life. But I have a gun. And I will shoot you if you're in my house at three a.m. without an invitation. And I don't have any issue with that. Now, most people don't know that. I've said it. But they don't hear it.

I like my animals. I take care of my animals . . . but I do wear my fur coat sometimes. I'm a wealth of contradictions.

Sue me.

I don't believe in the death penalty. Unless you touch a child. And then, you shouldn't even get a trial. Oh, but wait! Here's why that's wrong. Not too long ago, there was a gentleman who had been in jail for thirty-five years for molestation. And he never touched that kid. And what was he like when he got released? Forgiving. Because he felt that getting angry wasn't going to help him. He's right. If you're screaming, people generally stay away from you. But if you're speaking in a normal tone, people sort of start to hear and say, "Wha—? Whaaat?" Then you've reached someone.

So I'm wrong and the law is right. I guess folks do have to have a trial.

More contradictions, huh? What's next, needing warrants before you can wiretap American citizens? No, calm down . . . That would be crazy.

Anyway, don't assume you know someone.

And it's not just about folks in entertainment. In your own life, in your own neighborhood—you never know what's going on in somebody's house. People who think they know all about the neighbors across the street are dead certain they have them pegged. They say, "Those people over there? I'm sure what they're doing is running a meth lab." Or "That divorcée is one hot mess on the make." Well, they don't know . . . do they?

Just check out the neighbors we always see on the news when they find out that quiet guy upstairs is a serial killer or was imprisoning kids he and his nice wife had kidnapped. They all say how blown away they are. Like they never had a clue. Because they don't. Or, on the other hand . . . you have those noisy rabble-rousers . . . folks who dress all scruffy and park on their front lawn. And you don't know it . . . but they're donating their weekends at a hospice or something.

You don't know. And if you're not really interested in taking the time to find out, then don't talk about it. It goes back to:

THE THREE QUESTIONS:

Does it put any food on your table?
Does it enhance your life in any way?
Does it affect your personal being?

Got it? Good.
Now. I wonder what Simon Cowell is really like . . .
God, am I a walking contradiction, or what?

Commonly Used Hurtful Words and Phrases

Stupid

Dummy

Idiot

Retard

Lame-o

Spazz

He or she takes the short bus

Cup o' Joe

White trash

That's so ghetto

You're so gay

Raggin' on somebody

And this is just a start . . . Add your own.

You Realize I Can Hear You

Remember how I said before, I could see you? I want you to realize I can now hear you too.

It's tough getting some people off their habits. Not smoking or drinking . . . That's easy. I'm talking comfort zones. Those things are armor plated. People get in them, and do they ever get stuck. If you don't believe me, ask someone to be more sensitive about their word choices. They turn all cranky and go, "These days you can't say anything."

But look around . . . Have you noticed? It is a newer day. We have to be conscious of the fact that the old ways don't flow the way they used to. Neither do the old words.

Take "Cup o' Joe." Now when you grab a stool at the diner and want some coffee, you might be thinking, "What sounds more friendly than asking for a nice, hot Cup o' Joe?" Well, maybe you didn't know the origin of that nickname for coffee goes back to the 1800s when a Stephen Foster song became popular. The name of the song? "Old Black Joe." I'll wait while you do the math on why some people might not like hearing that. Didn't take long at all, did it?

You hear people say "white trash" all the time. It's meant to insinuate that you are a white person who is not good enough . . . that you are garbage.

"That's so ghetto." Kind of the same thing, different flavor, don't you think?

Racism seeped its way into our culture, and now that it's in there, it's hard to get out. Back to habits and comfort zones . . . Think of all those vintage cartoons, the ones where all you see is black people in demeaning and stereotypical roles. You also see it in the cartoon portrayal of Japanese people in the World War II era. I love the Three Stooges, but they had black stereotypes too. The black cook would get bug eyes and see a "Guh-guh-guh-ghost." Or say, "This house sho' nuff gone crazy" . . . right before he ran out of the kitchen in a cloud of dust. Same with the Marx Brothers. Watch *A Day at the Races*.

Once these words and images go unexamined . . . they slide into the American language . . . and we all start using them. And not just racial stuff. How many times on a sitcom have you heard someone say, "That's retarded"? Or radio talk shows where someone calls someone else "a retard." Next thing, kids are calling each other that. And there we go . . . New habits are forming.

If you have a child with special needs, you already know "retard" is a derogatory term meant to insinuate that somehow that person is "less than." It's all about ridicule. And marginalizing. They're not only using it to belittle the person they are calling retarded . . . who probably isn't . . . but they are also stigmatizing people with special needs, who, frankly, aren't getting much benefit out of the contribution, thank you very much. But people do it. Without thinking.

Even me. I'll cop to it right here . . . I'm guilty of this too. I've used the word "retard" in the past, not really thinking of its harm. But then a friend of mine asked me what another friend of ours who had a special needs kid in her life would think if she heard me say that. Busted.

Sarah Palin wanted President Obama's chief of staff, Rahm Emanuel, fired for telling a meeting that some plan they had cooked up was "fucking retarded." I do admit *one* of those words really bothers me.

Saying so-and-so "takes the short bus" is code for "he's retarded." They get that term from the smaller, special needs school buses, you see. It's just another way to marginalize and stigmatize.

Besides, I like those bitty little buses. I see them zipping around and say, now there's a cool ride.

Is it me, or in what world is telling someone "You're so gay" meant to be anything but a put-down? Like that is something not to be? Look, we can debate the pros and cons of gay marriage and gay rights all you like . . . but when you slam someone simply for who they are as a person . . . you're just being plain hurtful.

Some women are offended by the word "ragging." As in, "She's been ragging on me." It's all about a woman's period and hormonal crankiness—and comes from the slang for sanitary napkins. If folks are offended, why use it—unless you are trying to be mean? And you aren't . . . are you?

A comment Senator Harry Reid made years ago came back to haunt him. Somebody dug out an embarrassing sound bite when he described the prospects for Barack Obama to succeed as a Presidential candidate . . . Now, you have to understand, Reid was speaking in support of then-senator Obama when he described him as "light-skinned" and that he was an African American "with no Negro dialect, unless he wanted to have one." Senator Reid apologized. And the President accepted it and moved on. But it's one more marker that shows us race is a tough topic. And how to discuss it . . . That is something we now have to deal with because, guess what? We do have a black President.

And now that we have a black President, we need to be prepared for . . .

A female President
A Hispanic President
An Asian President
A Native American President
A gay President
A lesbian President
A transgender President

So, all manner of describing people has to change. Phrases that we never thought of as derogatory . . . well, they will have to be examined and gone over and explained. And if you are the party that chooses to utter those names or expressions . . . you're going to be called up or called out.

Does retard mean retarded?

Do you need to rethink your vocabulary? Chances are, yes.

Words do mean something.

But there are two categories here: people who say things to hurt; people who inadvertently say things that hurt.

So what do we do about all this stuff that's getting said and offending so many people? Sarah Palin wanted Rahm Emanuel to get the boot. Mark the date and time. I think she is correct . . . that what he said isn't acceptable. *However* . . . every offense does not warrant a firing.

Sometimes a swift kick in the pants will do.

See, that's where consequences come in. If there are no consequences for somebody's action, then people think it's OK. But there should be consequences for it. If you get punched in the nose because you called somebody lame-o, you're probably not going to do it again.

But what we need is less capital punishment for words, and more thinkable moments. Otherwise, from what I hear out of folks' mouths . . . pretty soon, we'd have to fire everybody.

The Smarter Things to Say

If you need to get your licks in, there may be a smarter way to say the same thing without lowering yourself into the word sewer.

Sure, it's kind of a hassle to think all this through rather than go for the old cheap shot. But hey . . . that's what makes you the smarter person.

And . . . if all else fails . . . "asshole" is still kind of fun.

Offensive Language

Have you recently made fun of someone by using an offensive term?
    If no, score 0
    If yes, score 5

Is it bothering you that you did?
    If yes, score 2
    If no, score 5

*Is it possible that you hurt somebody or taught someone else
it's OK to do the same thing?*
    If you think yes, score 5
    If you think no, score 2

Do you care?
    If yes, score 0
    If no, score 5

Would it piss you off if they said it about you?
    If yes, score 5
    If no, score 10

Total score: _____

Tally your score and write it in on the Master Score Sheet
at the back of this book, page 195.

Think It, Don't Say It

There's an old joke about this guy named Joe. Joe was having a terrible, hard life full of one tragedy after another. After years of this, the poor guy finally has had enough and climbs to the top of a mountain. Joe stands there on the summit and cries out to the heavens, "Why God, why me?" And the clouds part and the voice from above booms, "Because, Joe, you fucking piss me off."

God gets a lot of great jokes, have you noticed that? But what are you going to do? It's God.

Now without the "fuck," that joke isn't so funny.

Unless . . . unless the delivery is exceptional. And the "fuck" is subtext. So it can still be funny . . . Just think the "fuck."

Think the "fuck," don't say it.

You try it.

"Because, Joe, you . . . Piss. Me. Off."

I wonder how many fights could be avoided, how many hurt feelings would be spared, if people just didn't say every little thing that came into their heads. Hey, we all think nasty things. But saying them? I dunno . . . The wrong word to the wrong person at the wrong time can turn ugly in a hurry. The beauty is, you can still think it. Just don't let it come rolling out of your mouth.

And that's something that I've had to learn on *The View*. I have to think it. Say it with a look. Or shade the meaning when I say something so you just *know* I am thinking that word . . . but not saying it.

After all, it is Daytime TV.

Now that you know my secret, you can enjoy the show on a whole new level. But a word of caution. Don't assume every time I look thoughtful, that's what I'm thinking. 'Cause sometimes when I look like I'm thinking . . . it's just gas.

Things to Think and Not Say

The world does not need another fight. Especially if you start it. Look around, there's enough SOBs with no manners out there jump-starting arguments by slipping out with the wrong words. Don't you be one of them.

All you have to do when you talk to people who push your buttons is to be cool. Just be a better actor.

- Think the "fuck," don't say it.
- Think the "what an asshole," don't say it.
- Think the "I could deck you with one punch," don't say it.
- Think the "no way those boobs are real," don't say it.
- Think the "dipshit," don't say it.
- Think the "slut," don't say it.
- Think the "you're drunk," don't say it.
- Think the "scumbag," don't say it.

You get the idea. It's the best of both worlds. You don't swear, but you sort of do. You sort of stealth swear by just thinking it.

And next time you see me sitting there, just smiling quietly, you don't have to worry about me. I'm just busy thinking.

Buddy Is the New Nigger

Have you noticed how rarely we have a conversation about race in this country? I think the whole race thing hits a raw nerve.

BUT... Get out the Advil, because we're going to have one now.

Racial to me in my age group, and racial to other people, may mean two different things. Like people under the age of thirty. They don't get what you're talking about when you're saying, "That's racist." They say, "Well . . . what's racist?"

The word "nigger," to my granddaughter, does not mean what it means to my grandmother. That word does not have the same connotation. Know what's happened? The kids were smart. They took it out of the realm of insult and made it . . . familial.

If you're not black, how many times have you been waiting in a line, or in a coffee shop, or hanging around near black people and were surprised to hear them call each other nigger? Come on, sure you were. And I'm betting it wasn't just once. Not even just once in a sentence. It's like, ". . . And so I said, 'Nigger, what's going on . . .'" "Come on, nigger, I'm not going to do that . . ." "Nigger, you crack me up."

The word may not mean to him what it means to other people. It's a term of endearment to him. It's familial. Fraternal. He was using it like saying, "Hey, buddy."

Buddy is the new nigger.

I told a joke on a Bravo special because they had just buried the word "nigger." And I said, "Well, I want you to tell me if this joke is funny. And if it's funny because the word 'nigger' is in it . . . or if it's just a funny joke. So I will tell you the joke."

A little black cherub is up in heaven and is kind of cruising around, and God comes walking by, and the cherub flies over and says, "Hi, God!"

God says, "Hey, how are you doing?"

The cherub says, "Fine. God, can I ask you something?"

"Sure," says God.

"Am I an angel?"

God says, "No, nigger, you a bat."

Now, do you think that's funny? . . . OK, but what makes it funny? Is it the word "nigger" that makes it funny, or is it the idea that God is walking around heaven and some little cherub wants to know if he's really an angel, and God, in His infinite wisdom, says, "No, idiot, you're a bat."

So what makes the joke funny?

The right word . . . and you can't pretend you don't know it is.

It's like "Take my wife—please." You kill the joke if it's "Take my wife." See, to me, the "take my wife" is not funny. It's the "please" that gets me. So it is the word. It is the right word.

But see, now, this is what I'd say to you. There are times when racial jokes are funny. I know it's bad to say that, but it's true, and I hate, hate, hate to laugh . . . but I do.

And people freak themselves out over the angel joke because it *is* funny. It's a funny joke. But on that special they freaked out because they didn't know *why* they were laughing. They didn't know whether they were laughing because I said "nigger" in the joke, or because it's an angel. They didn't know. And so, if you were watching when I told it, you saw people go HA! And then recoil and cover their mouths.

But, come on, it's funny.

Am I right, buddy?

Just Because I'm a Catholic, Don't Assume That a Priest Has Touched Me

Were you around in the 1970s to watch one of the great TV series, *The Odd Couple*? There was this line in one episode that was so cool, I'll never forget it. You can still hear folks quote it. Check out the Internet, you can even find the clip floating around there. It went like this . . . Felix Unger was warning someone about assuming things. His line was, "You should never assume, because when you assume, you make an ASS of U and ME."

Brilliant!

But I have to ask, why are we all still doing so much assuming?

Example? How about the Tiger Woods situation? You have the incident that Thanksgiving night at his place in Florida. The story is that he comes out and he hits a fire hydrant and a tree. Then a rumor flies around that he and his wife were fighting about another woman. And then a rumor comes out that there are other *women*. And then all these women start showing up. We all pretty much know about the rest. The separation, the sex rehab, the press conference, the divorce decision. We don't need to get into all that.

What we do need to remember is this . . . What the Tiger story was all about for months—months—was rumor. And speculation. And, wait for it . . .

Assumption.

Folks were assuming he was doing this. Folks were assuming his wife was doing that. They were assuming he was in seclusion. Then they were assuming he was on his boat. Folks were assuming everything, and you know why? Nobody knew.

Look, whether it's Tiger Woods, or Governor Somebody, or that neighbor or nice aunt who suddenly checked into rehab, here's what we need to remember. Nobody really knows what happens in a personal situation except the people involved. But that doesn't stop anybody from assuming. Making ASSes of U and ME . . .

Well, I'll tell you what we should be doing instead. We should be saying, "We don't know. 'Cause we're not there."

So it sells newspapers to put the pictures of some chick on the cover with the screaming headlines saying this is the woman, and all. But the bottom line is:

. . . And?

For me, I want to ask those "journalists" why they try to give me information that they don't actually *have*—and call it news. And why am I accepting of that as fact? People would have much less to talk about if they had to stick to the facts. And then what the hell would the tabloids do?

The reputable newspapers have a policy of verifying facts with independent sources. Doesn't mean they always do it. But that's what they're supposed to do. And then it makes you wonder—or should—what it means when they report something but won't name their source. When they do that, they say they're reporting news, but what they're really saying is this is what we *hear* happened. Look for the wording. It's usually something like, "A source close to this says this is what happened." Or "Sources with knowledge of the situation indicate . . ." Hey, if you trust your newspaper or news station . . . that may be all right for you. For the reputable media, what they are doing is using careful language to say that they have done their homework and have verification. They just can't name the names.

But not all media are to be trusted. I *know*. Can you believe that?!?

And even the trustworthy newsrooms are cutting back so much on staff that the verification can get sloppy. They mean well but don't have the bodies to do the homework. And then it goes out.

And these days, once you put it out there, it's out. It's out there for a lifetime. And it doesn't matter whether it's true or not. It doesn't matter what the innuendo is. Hell, for some, innuendo isn't shameful . . . it's their specialty. They should have promos that say, "We're your twenty-four-hour source for rumor and innuendo!"

Innuendo sticks . . . sticks like bus station TP to the bottom of your shoe. Smells about as good too.

There was plenty of innuendo with Michael Jackson. The frowning newscasters with the big voices said, "The FBI followed Michael Jackson for seventeen years." And the people watching TV all nod and say, "Uh-huh . . . You know what *that* means, don't you?" No, I don't know what that means.

The FBI also followed Dr. King. They also followed John Lennon. Yeah, they followed a lot of people. And, as I understand it, Michael had one trial and he was acquitted. Now, some people say he paid someone twenty million dollars. Well, what was he paying twenty million dollars for? To keep them quiet? Obviously that couldn't have been all. So maybe he was paying twenty million dollars to just have them stop messing with him.

I don't know. Know why? Because I wasn't there.

So unless we were there, we can't take it at face value. Unless we were in the house with Tiger and his wife, or unless we spent time with Michael . . . unless we were there . . . we don't know.

We can only assume.

Ask Felix Unger what he thinks of that.

Oh, wait . . .

There Aren't Enough Jails

Picture this. Some guy driving the car in front of you is just sitting there after the light turns green, not moving. So neither are you. He's got his head down in that "I'm texting" pose. Five seconds pass. Ten seconds. Somebody leans on the horn but he's still too busy thumbing an urgent message about the egg salad he had for lunch. Wouldn't it be great if—Bam!—a cop shows up and yanks him out of the car and takes him away to jail. And the jail is right there, of course, so we could all see and enjoy it.

Wouldn't it be great?

Maybe this would work: For a minor infraction—you know, the bad manners–bad hygiene–bad language stuff—we could do what they do in hockey. Blow a whistle and stick the selfish jerk in a penalty box for a short period to reflect on his assholian behavior. Yeah, but those things would fill up awfully fast . . . So maybe not.

It's one thing to get pissed off at folks who transgress. The problem is what to do with them.

Don't we believe that the punishment should fit the crime? Isn't that what justice is? Lately, though, I wonder if we've gotten more into vengeance than justice.

I got thinking about all this when Ted Haggard and his wife, Gayle, were on *The View* one day. In case you don't recall, he was that evangelical minister who got caught up in a scandal. Hm . . . guess I'd better be more specific. His was over accusations of homosexual behavior and drugs. If I say "meth and massages," does that ring a bell? Thought so.

Anyway, hearing the Haggards talk about their lives now, and how they, along with their five kids, had fallen on hard times, got me thinking about the belief of Christian forgiveness . . . and how none of it seems to have gone to him. Not by his own congregation. He was cast out and now is scrambling to make ends meet. Couldn't they have just sent him away for a year to rehabilitate? Instead, he was kicked out with a small severance and gets nothing more from his church in support. This was the pastor of a Christian church.

Is there any forgiveness? If somebody does something wrong, we now have copped this "off with the head" attitude, which, I confess, feels *great* sometimes, but come on. Why do we paint everyone with the same brush? Why does it seem more and more we want people ruined rather than rehabilitated?

We do forgive some people. Even if it takes a while . . . But we do.

Richard Nixon is getting cut some major slack these days. Back then, what does he have . . . ? He has his Watergate burglary and cover-up. He gets rid of the tapes. He resigns before he is impeached and leaves office in disgrace. But while Nixon was president, he was a foreign policy genius. He opened China. Engaged the Russians. Give the man that. Thirty years later, he is no longer the villain he was. A major movie is made about him. His statements are put in a new context. We have sympathy for him as a man. Richard Nixon . . . oh yes, he wasn't so much a bad man as misguided, and awkward. Oh, yeah and sweaty-lipped. People forgive him.

Ronald Reagan didn't have all of Nixon's baggage, not even close, but there were plenty of folks who didn't like him a bit. He talked the talk all right. He told us it was "Morning in America" and accepted his second nomination: ". . . Recognizing the equality of all men and women, we are willing and able to lift the weak, cradle those who hurt, and nurture the bonds that tie us together as one nation under God."

. . . But wasn't he the one who let people out of the asylums, creating a homeless crisis? And busted the air-traffic controllers? And gave no AIDS help? And tried to get ketchup classified as a vegetable in school lunches? And wasn't his solution to the hole in the ozone layer to tell people to wear hats? And didn't he have his scandal too, the arms-in-exchange-for-hostages "enterprise"?

I'm just asking 'cause now he's revered. No one cares that he screwed up thousands of lives. They're talking about bumping President Grant off the fifty-dollar bill and putting Reagan on it. OK. I have a feeling the people who didn't dig Reagan won't be seeing a lot of fifty-dollar bills anyway.

We forgive sometimes, and sometimes we don't. One thing that's consistent is, at least in the early going, we love to punish and we need to find a villain.

Is everybody a villain? Or do we need to back up and draw some distinctions here?

THE TRANSGRESSORS

The people who have transgressed fall into two categories. First . . . true *villains* for whom there is no forgiveness. In my book, there are:

THE ASSHOLES:

Hitler
Stalin
Osama bin Laden
Saddam Hussein
Idi Amin
Augusto Pinochet
Timothy McVeigh
Mussolini
Charles Manson
Lee Harvey Oswald
James Earl Ray
Sirhan Sirhan
Ted Bundy
John Wayne Gacy

Jeffrey Dahmer

Richard Speck

Richard Ramirez

Boston Strangler Albert DeSalvo

Balkans war criminals Karadzic and Milosevic

Canadian pig-farm serial killer Robert William Pickton

The Connecticut home invasion killers (alleged)

Charles Whitman

Mark David Chapman

Reverend Jim Jones

Ft. Hood shooter (alleged) Nidal Malik Hasan

Truck bombers, including of the U.S. Marine dorm
   in Beirut

Virginia Tech shooter Seung-Hui Cho

FBI traitor Robert Hanssen

Bernie Madoff

. . . and so on.

We're talking about context.

Villains are vilified.

Can you really put villainy in the same context as . . .

ASSHOLIAN BEHAVIOR:

Michael Vick

Tiger Woods

Charlie Sheen

Jon Gosselin

Jimmy Swaggart

Ted Haggard

Pistol-packin' Washington Wizards players
   Gilbert Arenas and Javaris Crittendon

Plaxico Burress

Balloon Boy's parents

Pat Robertson

Rush Limbaugh (for the Haiti comment)

Heidi Fleiss

Pete Rose

Mark McGwire, Sammy Sosa
   (and all of the 'Roidian Slicks in sports)

South Carolina Governor Mark Sanford

Eliot Spitzer

Ex-Senator Larry "Wide Stance" Craig

Andy Dick

Jesse James

Whoopi Goldberg

Or . . .

Your name here?
         . . . Just asking.

Take Your Stinking Paws Off Me, You Damned Dirty Ape!

I don't like to be touched . . . I mean by strangers . . . And people who have no business doing it. If we have that kind of relationship where we can be touching and squeezing and rubbing each other, you would be the first to know it. And it would be wonderful.

But we don't have that relationship, so don't presume it.

I don't understand why it is that so many complete strangers are so touchy-feely all the time. There are basically two kinds of touchers, I think. People who have no sense of boundaries . . . and people who violate boundaries and don't give a rat's ass.

But wait, Whoopi, you say. Aren't some folks just warmhearted nurturers who not only mean you no insult, but on the contrary, are offering their touch as a gift? Do you want to have an issue with someone who is sharing their warmth through physical contact?

Yes. Because they assume an intimacy we do not have. It's bad manners wrapped up in a bear hug.

Still makes it bad manners to me.

Some folks will introduce themselves to you with an embrace that should be reserved for their wedding nights or dance club grinding. Or some come up behind and tug your elbow at the dinner table. Or try to say something they think is funny, and to make sure you are enjoying their joke . . . they'll vise grip your forearm and give it a squeeze. Or sock you on the shoulder. Or shake your hand and will *not* let go. They talk and smile and keep squeezing . . . and squeezing . . .

If you are one of these clutchers and don't know it—you do now. Think about it. Do you know you are doing it? Now that you read this, maybe you do.

Respectfully? Please stop . . . Please? If it's cool to cross that physical line with a person, they will let you know.

And unless you are the Savior Almighty . . . and you are invited . . . don't touch. Same goes for touching pregnant ladies. *Ask*, and most mothers-to-be will tell you how creepy it is to have folks both known and unknown to them placing one hand, and sometimes even two, on their bellies.

To be real clear, I'm not talking about some display of warmth from a soul mate. No, this is something else. And whether it's an unwelcome sexual come-on, or some kind of display of power, or just some warm and fuzzy personal contact . . . unless this is the day spa and I have hired you for a licensed massage . . . don't touch.

Thank you. Now give yourself a hand.

But just yourself.

The Hands-Off List

To help you respect personal boundaries, here are a few touching behaviors to avoid:

- Unwanted hugs

- Tugging sleeves or elbows

- Prolonged or intimate hugs

- Touching pregnant bellies

- Boob grazing. You fool no one.

- Arm slugging

- Arm squeezing

- Lint picking

- Hair fixing

- Tickling

- "Free" shoulder massages

- Leaning

- Goosing

Behavior to Avoid
in the Workplace

Beyond the obvious legal and ethical boners, you know, small things like embezzlement, fraud, misappropriation of funds, corporate spying, toxic dumping, and gunplay are the day-to-day, ground-level behaviors that you might want to stay away from at work. Things like:

- Gossip

- Office politics

- Desk snooping

- Boisterous behavior in an open office

- Sexual harassment

- Stealing food from the office fridge

- Leaving your rotten food in the office fridge

- Trashing the break room with your mess

- Taking the last of the coffee and leaving it empty

- Using the last of the copy paper and leaving it empty

- Eavesdropping on your workmate's conversations

- Ignoring emails and phone calls

- Being late, disrespecting other people's time

- Chewing out a coworker in a group setting

- Making fun of a coworker when they aren't there

- Lying

- Lying about lying

- Taking credit for someone else's work

- Shifting blame from your failed work

- Blatant ass-covering

- Secretive ass-covering

- Ass-kissing, both blatant and secretive

- Sneaking smokes in the office or bathroom

- Getting on the elevator reeking of smoke, perfume, or cologne

- BO is no picnic either

Simple Requests for Portraying Black People

If you are making a movie, or a TV show, or a play, or a book with black characters in it, please remember:

It's a baby's mama, not a baby mama.

There is a *k* in "ask." There is no *x*.

And there are tenses: past, present, and future.

I asked.

I ask.

I will ask.

I repeat, there is a *k* in "ask," not an *x*. An ax is something you chop wood with. Unless you're an ax murderer. And if you do need to chop some wood, you don't ax to use the ax.

And please put the consonants in all of our words. Especially a letter *g* at the end of words that have them . . .

. . . If that's not axin' too much.

Questions You Should Ask a Week Before Guests Come to Your House

- Are you allergic to cats?

- Are you allergic to dogs?

- Does cigarette smoke bother you?

- Does marijuana smoke bother you?

- Do orgies bother you?

Be a good hostess. This is good behavior that makes everybody happy.

Who Rules When It's Not Your House?

Every house has its own rules. Some families are strict about some things . . . others not. What's OK and not OK in my place may not be the same at yours. Kind of makes the world go round, doesn't it? But that also creates a sort of . . . rules gap . . . and when your kids get older and start spending more time out of your house and in other people's . . . it can be a problem. It's usually a bigger deal if you are a parent with many rules and your child is having, say, a sleepover, at a house that runs a little looser.

The thing is, you've got to figure the other parents are not going to honor your rules when it's not your house . . . They're just not. And your kid is not going to tell you they're breaking your rules if another parent says it's all right. Now . . . you can say, "Listen, different families have different rules. When you are over there for your sleepover, you tell them you're not allowed to watch R-rated films." And the other parents, who think the R-rated film is just fine, will probably go, "Well, it's OK, I'll talk to your mother."

They're never going to talk to you about it. Never.

But here's what you say to your child. "Lots of graphic violence might not be what you need to see. You might not need to see people having sex. You might *want* to see people having sex, but you don't need to see it if you are thirteen years old. 'Cause sex will come around. So this is one of those situations where you're at somebody's house, and . . . unless they're offering you alcohol—which is a definite no . . . you're going to have to figure out how you want to play it. And I'm going to trust you to know what to do. Because now you're having sleepovers and you're at someone else's home. Just know when you bring your friends over here, we're not going to do that. We're not going to be watching those things. And we're going to be going to bed at eleven or midnight."

It's a tough thing to say to a kid, "You're going to have to make a decision. And let me know what you decided. Just because I'm curious." But . . . that's empowering to a young person. If you make it OK for them to tell you that they've done something, they'll always tell you because it's not scary for them to do it. Because it's encouraged.

"Just let me know. And it'll be something you made a choice about. Now, I might ask you why you chose that . . . or why you chose this . . . but it's a discussion. Because I raised you to really know where the line is. You watched an R-rated video? OK. You're the one that's going to have the nightmares. You smoked pot? That's an issue. You know that's not what we're doing at thirteen. But if that's happening, you need to let me know . . . So I can decide whether I want you to be over there if they get arrested. As opposed to having to come get you from jail."

My kid was fourteen or fifteen when she got pregnant. I'm the first person she told. Now, she knew I wasn't going to like it. But our relationship was such that she could tell me whatever's happening and we'd figure it out. But she knew she didn't need to be afraid of me. Or that I was going to be so mad that I was going to put her out.

And for me, that was a great thing, that she told me. And that she wasn't afraid that I was going to do something 'cause she chose to do something that I would have suggested she wait to do. But kids . . . when they're out there . . . kids make some bad decisions. Or not smart decisions for the time.

Now, I like the kid that she had. But did she need to have a kid at fourteen, fifteen? No.

And when I said to her, "What's the plan, what do you want to do? Because if you're old enough to go out and do this, you must know what your plan is." And she said, "I want to have this baby," and I said, "OK, I wish you'd double think it, just because you're so young . . . but we'll be there to help you." Because that's what choice is. Choice is just deciding what *I* think is best.

But I told her, "If you decide you're going to have it, then I support you. Both emotionally and financially."

That's what defines a family. It's forever, it's unconditional. If you bring a kid into the world, I think it has to be unconditional. That's the one rule.

Noisy Neighbors

Unless you live on a farm, you're going to hear your neighbors. In the suburbs, they may not be as on top of your life as they are in an apartment building, but sooner or later, you're going to get annoyed by some racket some neighbor is making at the wrong time for you.

What's on your list? Leaf-blowers on Saturday morning? Late-night carpentry in the garage workshop, complete with routers and power saws? Playing that drum kit at all hours? Loud parties?

Well, I've done all those things. I'm not necessarily for all that, but I get it. And if you're doing all that, and not thinking too much about the noise you're making for your neighbors, you don't know that you're a bonehead.

So, here's what I want to say to you . . . Just think about it. Think about whether you want to be playing those drums at four in the morning. But at the same time, when you're drunk, you think you're cool. And you think you *really* play the drums well. Hey. FYI . . . If your last name isn't Starr? You might want to check.

Think about whether belt-sanding that door can wait until daylight. Or if the leaves can stay on the driveway until people have at least had a cup of coffee. As for the loud parties? Tough call. Who has a party that stops at ten p.m.? I mean, really? Isn't that when most folks are just getting there?

And if you're the one being bothered by the noisy neighbors, here's what I want to say to you. As much as I wrote this book to talk about some of the annoying behaviors that are bugging the piss out of us in our crowded-together lives, the idea isn't to become the Manners Cop of the World. Sometimes you just have to lighten up and accept the occasionally annoying things other people do as what you get with other people around. And how bad is it? Come on, honestly. How many late-night parties do you really have to deal with?

Want to retaliate? Here's what you do. Don't call the cops on them. You throw a party. And invite them. I would. Clearly they know how to have a good time.

The thing is, life's gonna happen and it's going to be annoying sometimes. But, hey, at some point, guess what? You're annoying too. So be a human being.

Try. It's not easy, but try.

Bullies

This is another one of those subjects that's worth a whole book on its own. And, as much as I don't want you to think I'm trivializing it by including it with stuff about, what . . . public nail clipping and cell phone yakkers . . . I trust you to be smarter than that. Because I believe you are. This book is all about behavior that bothers us. How can I not include a chapter on behavior that goes beyond that? Bullying goes way past peeve. But it's still bad behavior. And it's too much on my mind not to share here with you.

Now, I've always known that there were bullies in the world. We've seen a lot of it in politics lately as well as in daily life. You see it where people who may be stronger, or bigger, or better with verbiage than other folks . . . show off. To me, that's what bullying is, showing off. It's saying, I'm better than you, I can take you down. Not just physically, but emotionally.

I'm pretty sure a lot of teenage bullying comes from seeing adults and how they act around other people. How they put themselves out there. And I think that's where adults are involved . . . as poor examples to kids.

And for some reason, there seems to be no internal policeman for a bully that says maybe you're hurting somebody's feelings. Or worse, maybe you're going to push this person too far and they'll do something terrible. Something's not processing correctly in a bully's head. It doesn't seem to occur to them that what they're doing is crossing a line that shouldn't be crossed. And it's really, in my mind, no different than taking on defenseless kids. You do it just because you know you can.

It's an exercise in power, but it's also meant to disintegrate someone's Self. It's meant to take away their sense of who they are. And why? Because they're not as strong, or as big, or as witty.

Bullies are ball-less, soul-less creatures to me. And they're not just children, they're adults too. And have you noticed how they only bully people who won't fight back? You never see bullies try to bully other bullies. No bully wants to get his ass kicked. That's why so much of what they do . . . they do anonymously. Like throwing bricks through windows. That's bullying. Spitting on somebody is bullying. Yelling out "faggot" is bullying. And then they never stick around for the person to see them.

It's a terrorist act.

It's meant to make you feel afraid. It's meant to make you feel powerless to take care of the situation you find yourself in. And even when you try to, not enough adults take bullying seriously. Know what's clear to me? People don't realize that bullying has come so very far since many of us were little kids. Back then, if you ran into a bully, you could go get your big brother or big sister.

Today, you've got cyber-bullying. Cyber-bullying is different. First of all, it's very cowardly. The bully can choose to hide behind the anonymity of the Internet. And when bullying happens on the Web, it has no boundaries, so it's even more emotionally and psychologically charged. If you are the victim . . . you can't leave it behind at the bus stop or the hallway or the cafeteria. It's everywhere, and that's what I think makes cyber-bullying so much worse. It continues after the school day—and it gets broadcast.

Before the days of the Web and social networks, when you were getting bullied at school, it was just the kids at school who knew. But not kids in other schools. Not a million people around the world reading these things about you on the Internet.

And there's no way to combat the lie or fight the ugly once it's put out there. The ugly stays forever like a bad fart. It's always there. And you can't get it off the Internet.

I believe adults should step up and do more to stop this. But it's not getting done. Why is it that a kid can come and tell parents and teachers that this is happening, and everybody agrees it needs to stop—but nobody *does* anything? It reminds me of a famous New York news story from back in the mid-1960s. A young woman named Kitty Genovese was walking home from work one night, and she was attacked and stabbed. And she screamed and screamed and screamed. Her entire neighborhood heard it. Nobody helped her. A similar thing happened more recently in the Bay Area where a high school girl was gang-raped outside her school dance. A crowd of people stood by and nobody helped her.

What is missing that helping isn't even a second thought in people's minds?

What does a victim of bullying need to do to be heard? I mean, what better way is there to be heard than to walk up to the adults who are there in school to help the situation? Beyond that, where is there protection? If the adults don't give a damn, where are we?

I hear stories now that teachers are being bullied by students too. A common complaint is that they are told by kids right there in their classroom to fuck off. Well, here's a very good way to deal with them. If you say fuck off to a teacher in school, you get suspended. It's that simple.

It's like a child who won't behave on the train, and the mother quietly says, "Stop that. Quit it. Put that down . . . I'm coming over there . . ." And then the misbehaving continues and she does nothing. If you're going to deal with kids, you have to be ready to *deal* with them. You have to follow through and there have to be consequences.

I don't understand when it became OK for the kids to tell adults the rules. What does it say about us? What are we telling the kids? We talk all about the forms incivility takes today. I see bullying as the clearest example of how incivility is running amok.

I put a lot of it on the adults. You know, adults from just a generation or two ago would not have put up with that crap. If somebody came to 90 percent of those adults and said, "I'm getting bothered all the time, they're messing with me, and I've tried ignoring them, I've tried to fight back, and, you know, I'm *despondent . . .*" those grown-ups would have listened. Most adults back then would say, "OK, we're going down to that school right now and find out what's happening. And I'm going to talk to so-and-so's mother." And the kid would, of course, say, "No, no, don't do that! It'll make it worse." But the parent—the responsible parent—would say, "Well, I am going to talk to *somebody* and get to the bottom of this." It simply would not have been taken so lightly when a child came to you and said something was wrong.

And the adults in South Hadley, Massachusetts, where that bullied fifteen-year-old-girl committed suicide, seemingly were aware of it . . . So what the hell?!

You cannot ask children to respect anything if you're not going to respect it. If a kid comes to you and says, "I'm really having a tough time here," and you don't respect that enough to follow through, what is that saying to the *other* kids? It's telling them that nobody cares. It says to kids that they're out there on their own. And, as we have seen too many times, if you think you're out there on your own, and you think there's only one way to go, you kill yourself. And sometimes, other people.

And kids are not the only ones victimized by bullies. You can be thirty-five and messing with a bully. Bullies are bullies at any age or any place. But whether it's in school or at work, bullies are not acceptable. And that's something everybody has to just get on top of.

It's hard, I know it, but if you are a kid who is being bullied and harassed, here is what I want to say to you: I would find some grown-up who would listen to me and I'd make as much noise as I could. For me, there comes a time when it's *enough.*

It's the same in relationships, whether it's adults or if it's kids, where that person has that much power over you. So much that they can dictate what you're going to be doing. That's too much power to hand over to somebody. I feel very strongly that adults have to take a step back and take a look at this.

Please. Take a look at what it means.

What would it mean to you if someone bullied you at work? What would you do if you discovered on the company computer server that someone was spreading lies about you? But you can't figure out who it is. And people are giving you looks, and all that. And it's making your life miserable so you can't work, let alone sleep or eat. That's when you have to get up on top of the desk and go, "OK. I'm mad as hell, and I'm not going to take this anymore! I'm *not* going to do it!" It's OK to get mad and snap. It's not OK for someone to use someone else as a way to get their beans off.

The question is, why have people become so emboldened? Is it because the crowd that witnesses all this doesn't try to stop it? But that doesn't necessarily mean they like what the bully is doing. It could be that they are afraid too. But how can one bully hold more power than eight or nine people together? What happens if the bunch turns on the bully? People use this excuse all the time. "Oh, I didn't want to say anything because I didn't want them to start bullying *me*." Well, if you know that there are four other people who don't like what's happening, you have more power than the bully.

You have the power.

Besides kids getting examples set by adult bullies, what can we trace it back to? Is it what they see on TV? Is it the *Housewives of New York*, or *Beverly Hills*, or wherever? Is it Rush Limbaugh? Is it Keith Olberman? Is it these shows on TV like *Gossip Girl*, where the kids are just plain nasty? They're nasty about each other. They're nasty about other people who they perceive to be lower in the world than they are. They're characters with no redeeming qualities.

Why are we OK with that? Why don't we like people with redeeming qualities? When did that change? Maybe people with redeeming qualities are boring. But fewer people hurt themselves because of boring people, even though they're not "hot."

But ask yourself this. Are you actually hot when you're an asshole? Because it's basically what you are when you're a bully.

I think that both as kids and adults you kind of have to make a decision. How far are you willing to lie down for somebody? And as a parent, you cannot *be* your kid. You can't bring that vibe into the house like it's OK, we don't need to say anything.

Yeah, you do. You need to make noise when something is wrong.

But at the same time, that doesn't give you the right to be a bully yourself. If you look in the mirror and say, I'm getting bullied by somebody, therefore, I can bully, there's a problem and you could be looking at it in the eyes.

I don't exactly know how many bullies were once bullied themselves. It depends, I guess. If they got out of school and said, "That's never going to happen to me again, I'm going to go on the offensive," they could become bullies. If they got out of school and they said, "Oh my God, my life is always going to be like this," then, I suppose, they lie down.

But I have to say, in my opinion, if you're watching on the little kids' playground and you see your kid is a potential bully, that's when you have to nip that in the bud. It's not cool because there's your son—with his little penis and you with your big penis—and you think, yeah, he's standing up for himself.

Is he?

You may feel proud and say, "He's a fighter, that one."

Yeah, but who is he fighting? And who are you? What are you representing to your child? Again, it comes back to what makes this OK. When did it change that there was no policeman in your head saying, "You know what? That's really not a good way to go."

Is this going on because faith in the system at large has failed? Is it because people figure they're going to get theirs while the getting's good? Or thinking, nobody's gonna stop me?

But why not? Are teachers that busy? . . . Or are they that scared?

But then what? It's just lawless.

If you're not going to stand up and say, "*No fucking more*," not one more kid is going to have to go through this, then who is going to stand up? And if you, as a teacher, don't feel like you're strong enough to be in that classroom—because that's part of the teaching profession, to teach young people that this is not acceptable behavior—then maybe there's a better profession for you. And that's the bottom line of it, if you can't do the job. 'Cause the job is not just the numbers and the words and the letters on the blackboard, it's forming and shaping young people. Engaging them. And if you can't engage them enough to keep them from beating each other up, then you have anarchy in the school.

If you're afraid, and you know the kids are afraid . . . where do you go from there? Does it mean you have to make friends with the biggest, baddest dude on the football team? Maybe. Unless he's the bully. Which he probably isn't because he doesn't have to be. And he doesn't have the time.

Where *do* you go from there?

OK, here's an idea. You start a club. You say to young kids, "Listen, this is a club that's looking out for other students who may not have anybody walking with them. This is a club because when you get out in the real world you want to look after one another and you want to be looked after. You want to feel like somebody's got your back. Let's start it now."

Also, there's nothing stopping teachers from starting clubs like that for themselves to get some support. Have a teacher's meeting and say, "Who's afraid of their class? And can you identify the elements of your fear in your classroom? Who do you think is getting bullied? Who do you think is bullying?" Then you say, "OK, Mr. Principal, these are the kids we're afraid of. So we're going to start a new class—just for all of them. We're having Officer So-and-so come in. And he's going to take them to the penitentiary."

It's a field trip! It'll be just like *Scared Straight*!

You want to let people see what bullying is like? Take them to the pen. And then see what real bullying is like.

And then you say to them, "Now, this is what you guys do. Whether you're doing it on the Internet, or you're doing it physically or psychologically, this is what you're doing. Remember that feeling you had in the pen that he was going to mess you up? That's what it's like for other people with you. So put yourself in that other position. Now that you have been in that position, you know what it's like. Do you want other people to feel this?"

For some people the answer is yes. So those are the ones, you say, "OK, until you can get your shit together, you can't come to our school."

And the school administrators have to say to their parents, "Hey, listen, we don't know what you're going to do with your kid. But he gets one more shot. And you'd better get on this because, otherwise, he's going to be sitting on your lap at work with you. Take your kid . . . and leave. He can't be here. We're not going to allow this."

It's all about taking responsibility. But will we really do that? I wonder.

Why don't we have as much zeal about these terrorists, the terrorists of our children and our workplace and our lives? Bullies are *terrorists*. They make you live scared, that's what terrorists do. But why aren't we treating bullies the same way we treat terrorists?

And Google and MySpace and Facebook and all those places, why aren't they picking up on this? Why aren't there committees that are out there combing for this too, and alerting people? The police monitor Internet chat rooms for predators, why not for bullies? Is it too much work? It's not as much work as a funeral.

So if no one is going to take responsibility, kiss your kids very carefully every night.

Am I a Bully?

Is there a person you regularly make threatening comments to, or give intimidating looks to, at work or school?
    If no, score 0
    If yes, score 5

Does it make you feel better that you do this?
    If no, score 2
    If yes, score 5

Is it possible that you hurt somebody or taught someone else it's OK to do the same thing?
    If you think yes, score 5
    If you think no, score 2

Do you care?
    If yes, score 0
    If no, score 5

Have you ever posted or forwarded a hurtful comment about another person on the Internet?
    If no, score 0
    If yes, score 5
    If you did it anonymously, score 10

Do you only put others down when it is in front of a group?
    If no, score 0
    If yes, score 5

Would it bother you if someone did the same thing to you?

　　If yes, score 5

　　If no, score 5

Total score: _____

Tally your score and write it in on the Master Score Sheet
at the back of this book, page 195.

Manners Don't Take
a Vacation

I don't care whether you are staying at a Motel 6 off the interstate or at the Four Seasons on Maui . . . it can drive you nuts the way some people behave in a hotel. I don't mean inside their rooms. (Some of my behavior in a hotel room might raise an eyebrow or two.)

You have that look on your face that tells me you don't know what I'm talking about. Let me explain.

Vacations are for fun and business trips may be for more serious purposes, but they have one thing in common . . . Your hotel stay is going to be hell if the other guests in it are inconsiderate. One of the things that people have talked about . . . and I concur . . . is noise. Hotel guest noise bites the big one.

Actually, there aren't many hotel peeves that chap my behind. In fact, there are only two. Both involve noise.

Let me talk first about the doors slamming. Unless it's used to dramatically finish an argument—it's not cool. And for that to be cool, you have to use a British accent and say, "Good day, sir!" before you turn on your heel and slam that thing. Think about it. At home or at work, most of us close doors . . . not slam. But somehow, people think what happens in a hotel stays in a hotel. It doesn't. 'Cause clearly, a lot of people don't like it . . . And they're talking about it. The doors that lead from your room to the hallway seem to be bang-friendly.

Sometimes it's because of the air suck created by the breeze in the hallway. Sometimes it's because the doors are hung in such a way as to make sure they close when a guest leaves the room. So, yeah . . . they're *made* to close.

And they close loud enough—on their own—to rattle the water glass in the room up the hall. But when it slams . . . you wet your pants! Or, you're asleep and it wakes you up. Either way, it's not good.

OK, so we've learned that the design of hotel doors works against us, and here's how we combat the god of Slam. Rest your hand on the doorknob so the door closes instead of slams. Voila! And yet nobody does it. Maybe now they will.

The other hotel hell moment is loud talking in halls. The surest way to get people cussing someone out from within their room is some other someone walking the hotel corridor talking to the person right beside them like they were shouting over a jet engine. I mean, come on. There's no reason for this.

When adults do it, nine times out of ten, it's after the bars have closed. Hey, what are you going to do?

But sometimes, parents let their kids run wild in the halls. Hey, what kid on a vacation doesn't love to run? And there's that long, carpeted runway for them to just sprint down, or play tag on— shrieking in delight. Well, moms and dads, this is a chance to let your kids know what it is like to be out in the world—where there are things like rules, and manners, and consideration.

Independence is wonderful for children, and vacations are a good way to stretch their boundaries . . . but you've got to help them. I also know kids are going to want to be kids, and that's great. But they can be kids by the pool or on the beach and not right outside hotel rooms, where most people are craving peace and quiet.

Look, I'm not fooling myself. Just like the doors that are engineered to slam, I don't believe hotel hallways are suddenly going to becomes churchlike. But I can dream.

But not if somebody's noisy kids are outside my door.

May I Have Your Attention Please? . . . *Please?*

Have you tried to have a conversation with anyone these days and just end up feeling like you only have half their attention? It can happen when you're face-to-face with someone. Like at dinner when they keep doing that damn BlackBerry check. But know what drives me batty? When you're on the phone and you get those . . .

. . . long gaps . . .

. . . that make you think . . . that . . .

. . . the other per . . .

. . . son is not focused on you.

They can't see you when you are talking with them and so the temptation is simply too hard to resist when the computer . . . or the BlackBerry . . . or the iPhone . . . or the iPad . . . is calling out to them.

"Hey, baby! Come on and check me . . . You know you want to. Someone might be inviting you to a party! . . . Maybe there's news about that job you want . . . Come on, aren't you just dying to check the tweets to see what color underwear John Mayer says he's wearing today?"

And then the device takes hold of them. But the person on the other end is powerless. Because they don't know what this other person is doing. Because they're certainly not conversing. Which is what they should be doing if somebody calls them up and they answer.

Some telltale signs are the neutral "uh-huhs," which sound a lot like "yes, dear." But even worse are the long gaps and clickety-click of the keyboard you hear in the background from the person you thought was actually listening to you while you poured your heart out about the life-changing experience you had upon visiting the sick relative in the ICU who finally forgave you for joyriding in his car when you were fifteen.

. . . Hello?

Click, click, click. Tappety-tappety-tap . . . "Uh-huh . . . Riiight." Click, click . . .

While the phone mute button is sometimes necessary, that's not what I want to talk about. I want to talk about the unnecessary times. Times when you're talking along and when you pause, you hear a silence so dead it could be the atmosphere on Jupiter. And then a soft click and a rush of sound from the person you thought you were chatting with. Know what they did? They muted their phone so they could talk with someone else in the room or the office—and didn't tell you. Maybe it's only for a few seconds. But still . . .

Know what you can do about this? Want to have some fun? All right . . . Next time it happens and you know the other person was away, multitasking or chatting up somebody who walked in the room . . . here's what you do. When they finally do return to the line—pretending they didn't leave—say this: "Good, then, I'll just send the bill to you."

Then sit back and listen to 'em squirm. And while they try to figure out how to find out what the hell you were talking about, you can relax and enjoy their discomfort. Maybe even check your email.

Stress One Now

Don't you just love when you call a business to talk to somebody . . . to tell them your issue, your problem . . . to get that little "personal touch" . . . and instead, you get that Stephen Hawking digitized voice that lets you know it's a computer-automated operator?

Those robot operators (roboperators) . . . I hate them.

I can understand why they have them. Not only does it save costs in this bottom-line economy, but I suppose a lot of calls that come in are so easy to categorize that a live body doesn't need to sort out the subtleties of what callers want. If you want to make a reservation, you press one now. To cancel, press two. Fine.

Oh, come on now. You know this is just because they don't want to have to hire another person and have to pay them.

And doesn't it seem that, most times, not even one of the options they offer applies *in any way* to what you called to do? What if I don't want to make a reservation? . . . Or cancel one? What if I want to find out if there is a car rental desk at the hotel? Or if the noisy building demolition across the street is still going on?

Sometimes you get into those automated systems and it's like getting shot down some Rube Goldberg (no relation) chute into a maze of electronic twists, turns, and dead ends. It's especially nutty when the voice recognition technology isn't up to snuff and it can't understand what you are saying.

"If you are a current customer, say 'yes.'"

"No."

"So to confirm, you are a current customer, correct? If so, say yes."

"No."

"Good. I'll connect you to current customer relations. Your wait time is approximately . . . *horty-hoo inutes*." That's robot speak for "grab a comfy chair."

"But wait, I don't want—"

Click. And then you're enjoying the Soft Hits of the 70s.

Gaah!

If they're going to use these systems, they've got to get it together. How many times does the digital sweetheart ask you to input your account number, enter the date of purchase . . . and your middle school shoe size . . . only to have the live, warm body that finally comes on the line ask you for the exact same information all over again?!

Gaah! Gaah!

Since this is the wave of the future, rather than fight it and have steam come out my ears every time I call a business, I have learned to amuse myself with a little head game. It's simple. All you have to do every time you hear one of the little prompts of marketing bull, is to say the opposite in the operator's perky DJ voice. And try not to laugh. It's hard not to.

For example, when they say, "Your call is important to us," say, "You don't mean zip to us!"

"Thank you for your patience." You say: "You're a loser with nothing better to do!" And remember, keep it perky!

"Someone will be with you momentarily" becomes, "I hope you went potty, because this is going to take all day!"

"We're busy assisting other customers" translates to, "It's lunch hour, deal with it!"

All right, all right, it's not that much fun after the first twenty minutes. If you have a problem with that, just call. Because you *know* you are very important to us.

With All Due Respect

These were just things on my mind and some ideas of ways I could be better. Maybe it helps you too.

If not, pass this book on!

Master Score Sheet
for Self-Tests

Enter your numerical scores here for each self-test.

Parking =   _____

A Traveler Check =   _____

Resisting Textation =   _____

Stadium Behavior =   _____

Sideline Civility =   _____

Offensive Language =   _____

Am I a Bully? =   _____

TOTAL =   _____

What your score means:

If you scored between 0 and 30, your behavior rates as CIVIL.
Congratulations.

If you scored between 31 and 181, your behavior rates as
BORDERLINE BONEHEAD.
Oops.

If you scored between 182 and 259, your behavior rates as
ASSHOLIAN.
. . . Which means you probably don't care. But if you do happen to care? Back to page 1 and start over. We'll wait for you.
After all, it's the polite thing to do.

Glossary of Terms
& Other Words

Here are some of those terms that you came across in this book that I put together with a bit more definition and suggested usage. I've also added a few extras just for fun.

You probably have a few choice words of your own.

ASSHOLIAN: Behavior that could be seen as the renderings of a complete AH. But you are saved by your amateur status. You are human.

BIG BLOGGER: Allusion to George Orwell's *1984,* in which "Big Brother Is Watching You." Now the mysterious surveillance entity is the blog.

BLOGGARDS: A term blending bloggers and cowards, which, for the ones that hide behind anonymity, are pretty much the same. They are not worth much of your breath, so this nifty combo word keeps it short.

BONEHEAD: Having the quality of being a thoughtless pain in the ass. A good substitute for some of the other, more potentially hurtful things you call people. But then, boneheads are pretty much immune to offense. They don't get it.

BORG: Cyber-species from *Star Trek*. Borgs are followers, entities with a drone mentality against whom there is no resistance.

CRACKBERRY: Addiction to texting and email from your hand-held device. Not specific to BlackBerry users. An equal opportunity annoyance.

DADHEAD: A dad who is a sidelines jackass. Generally applied to those at youth sports fields and Little League bleachers, but tends to roam to various venues. Watch for him and his video cam at the next graduation.

DAILY REHAB: The ongoing process of trying to keep moving forward in your life. Hey, we all screw up. Or backslide. Here is where character kicks in and you do your work. Every single day.

DIGITAL RAGE, THE: Condition that is the byproduct of the Digital Age. We're antsy, impatient, angry, stressed, and otherwise hot and bothered over being so wired.

DUDEBAG: An only slightly milder way of calling a guy the word it sounds just like.

ELEVATOR EYES: An awkward condition that overcomes people when they get on an elevator with someone else and they can't manage to look at each other. So they look at anything they can find, usually changing floor numbers, with extreme fascination.

-IAN: Suffix you can add to the end of words to link the user with the condition. For example, asshole becomes assholian, as in, "Man, that is assholian behavior." Jackass becomes jackassian, and so forth.

PEERENT: A parent who tries to be a peer to his children or to their friends. The outcome is generally poor when nobody seems to be the adult.

REALITY CHICK: Woman famous for no discernable reason, except her reality show. Sadly, most aren't that famous. Maybe we're better off that way.

ROBOPERATOR: Those annoying robot operators that take our calls now instead of live people. Enjoy the perky voice. Dig the corporate smooth jazz on hold. Your wait time is . . . seeming like forever.

'ROIDIAN SLICK: Origin is athletes who cheated by using steroids (aka 'roids), but really applies to anyone who cheats his way to glory.

ROLE MORTALS: People we admire and look up to as role models, who are, in reality, all too human.

SOCCER MOBS: Soccer moms and dads who foster a mob mentality. They shout rude things and lose control on their kids' soccer sidelines. Related to: DADHEAD, above.

SOCIAL NETWORK SITE: Those fun places on the Web where everyone sees your personal business. Poster, BEWARE!!

STEALTH SWEAR: As in, think the curse, don't say it. Gives you the advantage of feeling good without all that pesky fighting after.

TALIBAN-ESQUE: Any behavior that imposes the beliefs of one person on everyone else. Conversations with the Taliban-esque are impossible. They aren't even conversations. With them, it's my way or no way.

TEXTATION: The overwhelming urge to text.

THE WTF LOOK: The expression that slowly grows on someone's face with the dawning unhappy realization that something bad is in the air. You see this a lot on airplanes and workplace kitchens when stinky food hits the fan. It's a look you don't want to get.